Go
Bananas!

May 2001

To Geoff, Banana Cream Pie...
Don't forget to eat your
bananas. Happy cooking.
Cheers!,
Susie Q

Susan
Quick

Go
Bananas!

150 Recipes

for America's

Most Versatile

Fruit

BROADWAY BOOKS

New York

BROADWAY

Broadway Books titles may be purchased for business or promotional use or for special sales. For information, please write to: Special Markets Department, Random House, Inc., 1540 Broadway, New York, NY 10036.

BROADWAY BOOKS and its logo, a letter B bisected on the diagonal, are trademarks of Broadway Books, a division of Random House, Inc.

Visit our website at www.broadwaybooks.com

Library of Congress Cataloging-in-Publication Data

Quick, Susan, 1959–
Go bananas! : 150 recipes for America's most versatile fruit / Susan Quick. — 1st ed.
p. cm.
Includes bibliographical references and index.
1. Cookery (Bananas) 2. Bananas. I. Title.

TX813.B3 Q53 2000
641.6'4772—dc21   99-059694

FIRST EDITION

Book design by Pei Loi Koay
Illustrations by Janet Pedersen
Banana leaves graphics by Roberto de Vicq de Cumptich

ISBN 0-7679-0403-6

00 01 02 03 04 10 9 8 7 6 5 4 3 2 1

This book is dedicated to Lola—
the best banana-eating vizsla dog in the whole wide world

Contents

Acknowledgments

I must confess that before writing this book bananas were not the fruit I reached for first, or even second. Plantains, to me, were those wonderful fried disks I ate at a little Chinese-Cuban restaurant I used to go to in Chelsea, but beyond that I had no real knowledge of this strange fruit. Do people in Puerto Rico really eat plantains three times a day? How on earth do you even peel them, let alone cook the funny looking things? Imagine my surprise as I found myself not only liking bananas and plantains but actually falling in love with so many dishes I discovered during the summer and fall I spent working on this book. I realized only recently that I hadn't eaten a potato the entire time, and never even missed them. Chances are, bananas are already *your* favorite fruit, and I hope trying some of these recipes will be as exciting and pleasurable a discovery for you as it was for me.

This is the place where everyone gets thanked, starting with my momma and my daddy, and my sister, Linda Combs, who serves double duty as my best friend.

I count my lucky stars for the day that I met Angela Miller, the prettiest and nicest (except when negotiating) book agent in the business. And

I had the great luck of having as my first cookbook editor the inimitable Harriet Bell—thank you, Harriet, for taking a chance on a fledgling writer and turning a quirky idea into a great little cookbook. My gratitude as well to Broadway editor Jennifer Josephy, who so ably picked up the reins and saw the book through its final stages, and to everyone at Broadway Books for their hard work and support throughout the project.

For my countless friends who kept in touch via phone and E-mail to offer their love, support, recipes, and research tips, I feel truly blessed. Alphabetically, they are: Lorraine Alexander, Toni Allocca, Karin Eaton, Valerie George-Ellis, David Greenbaum, James Hunter, Michael McCall, Susie Query, Lisa Rutledge, Alyce Smith, Sarah Smith, and last, but never least, Kay Shaw West.

Thanks as well to my countless guinea pigs and official tasters during the long, hot "summer of the banana" in Bucks County, Pennsylvania: Caleb Negron and Robert Triefus, Curtis Jensen, Cheryl Klauss, and Lewis Punlork Jensen, as well as the tableau of house guests and visitors cheerfully willing to try six desserts at a sitting.

I am especially grateful to my friends and mentors in the food world who lent their expertise and encouragement along the way: Sarah Belk-King, Mark Bittman, Giuliano Bugialli, Kerri Conan, Mitchell Davis, Dorie Greenspan, Lori Longbotham, Maria Robbins, and Bonnie Stern. Extra-special thanks with whipped cream on top to Mary Ann Howkins, a good friend and recipe tester extraordinaire.

The only thing better than getting to write your own cookbook is getting the best of all jobs in the food world at a wonderful magazine. I wish to thank all my *Real Simple* colleagues, especially managing editor Susan Wyland, Kay Chun, Rondi Cooler, MaryAnn DeSantis, Michele Fleisher, Sarah Humphreys, Barbara Jones, Carol Kramer, Maria Millian, and creative director Robert Valentine.

Lastly, I am deeply indebted to Ann Lovell, curator of the Banana Museum in Auburn, Washington, and a lovely person to boot. A banana devotee and a librarian, she graciously shared her wealth of resources with me. Everyone should be so fortunate.

Time flies like an arrow.

Fruit flies like a banana.

—GROUCHO MARX

Go
Bananas!

Introduction

How can you not love a banana? Just one bite and everything a banana has to offer—creamy texture, honeyed nectar—fills your mouth with delicious sweetness. Slice a banana over a bowl of yogurt, drizzle it with honey, top with crunchy granola, and you have a perfect breakfast. Freeze it, and it becomes a cool treat in summer or a soothing remedy for a teething baby. Whir it in a blender with ripe strawberries, orange juice, and ice cubes, and it's the smoothie of your dreams. Of course, it makes the best pie in the whole world—banana cream. And when your bananas are well past their prime, who hasn't mashed the pulp and turned it into a sweet bread?

Though most people think of bananas as a healthy snack or a way to add sweetness and fiber to their breakfast cereal, cooking bananas only makes them more luscious with endless possibilities. Fresh, sweet banana pulp can be added to soufflés, breads, and cakes, substituting for less-slimming fats and providing valuable nutrients as well as intense flavor. And that's just the tip of the banana, so to speak. Most of us consider bananas a starting point to a dreamy dessert, but to much of the world, it's dinner. Sautéed, baked, or grilled bananas

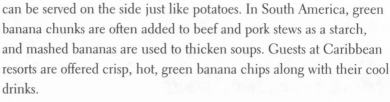

can be served on the side just like potatoes. In South America, green banana chunks are often added to beef and pork stews as a starch, and mashed bananas are used to thicken soups. Guests at Caribbean resorts are offered crisp, hot, green banana chips along with their cool drinks.

Because bananas and plantains are grown all over the tropics and subtropics, they are used widely in many of the world's cuisines. In Southern India, they are a staple food eaten at every stage of ripeness. When green, bananas are cooked as a vegetable and used in curries (even the skin is used). Once ripe, they are often turned into confections, jellies, and jams. In many countries the fruit is dried and processed into a flour used in breads and cakes. The male flower of some varieties is considered delectable and is cooked in a variety of dishes. In Myanmar, the national dish is *mohinga*, a fish soup with its essential ingredient being the inner soft heart of the banana trunk called *ngapyawoo*. Africans ferment the fruit to make beer which is drunk at festivals and used to toast the bride and groom at weddings. In Thailand, where banana plants on the grounds of Buddhist temples are considered holy, banana leaves are used as receptacles for steamed dishes, sweets, and for wrapping up raw foods in the market.

Bananas and plantains are one of the few fruits that can be eaten at all stages of ripeness. Plantains are synonymous with South American cooking and are treated like a vegetable, much as we use Idaho potatoes. In preparations ranging from fried plantain crisps called *tostones* to smoky-flavored *mofongo*, these oversize bananas are a staple for millions of people who rely on them for their everyday meals. Ironically, it's the sweet dessert bananas we're accustomed to in this country that many tropics dwellers tend to eat in moderation. Plantains are growing in popularity in this country due to greater interest in Caribbean, Cuban, Brazilian, and other Latin American cuisines. And many banana companies have increased their production to feed the frenzy.

Introduction

Once you've set aside the notion that bananas are only something to slice over your corn flakes or use in your grandmother's banana bread recipe, I hope you'll try them in the other breakfast dishes and quick breads in the following pages. And don't forget to pass banana appetizers at your next party or include them on the dinner menu—not to mention as the sweet finale. I encourage you to bravely forge ahead and peel a plantain to make wonderful spicy fries, or stir them into a simmering soup or stew. Trying out a new recipe is a way of learning about the many seductive flavors of the world's cuisines. Once you've experienced the variety of savory and sweet ways to cook this culinary chameleon, I hope bananas will remain your favorite fruit. So go ahead: Go bananas!

Banana Basics

Recently I listened with envy as a friend of mine, just home
from a trip to Indonesia, told of her adventures. She had spent much
of her time traveling from village to village, and each one seemed to
have a special variety of banana they were known for. Each fruit had a
unique texture and flavor: Some bananas were quite firm and tooth-
some, while others had an almost floury consistency. There were bananas that tasted of custard or lemons, while still others had berrylike
overtones. There were so many bananas that she lost track of how
many she had eaten. Her trip was measured in banana peels.

As my friend discovered, there are literally hundreds of varieties of
bananas—estimates range from 300 to 500. Most of us are familiar
only with the common staple Cavendish banana. But as more and
more tropical fruits and vegetables are being imported, a greater number of varieties are popping up—like the small, fragrant Niño, per-
fectly sized for children's little hands; and Red bananas from
Ecuador, which have a tangy aftertaste of raspberries (a personal favorite). These bananas vary not only in flavor but in ripening habits
as well. While the Cavendish banana can be eaten and enjoyed even

Bananas and Your Health

Bite for bite, bananas and plantains pack a lot of nutrition power. Raw bananas in particular are a great source of quick energy. (Have you ever noticed all the banana peels that marathon runners have to dodge in a race?)

Despite its rich, sweet flavor, a medium-size banana has only about 90 calories, is 99.5 percent fat free, and is high in Vitamins C, B6, and dietary fiber. Plantains, because of their high starch content, contain about two-thirds more calories than bananas, but have the same minuscule amount of fat. Plantains are a powerhouse of Vitamin A—they contain more than 1,800 IUs (international units)—and are also high in fiber as well as magnesium, Vitamin C, and folate.

Both fruits are quite high in the mineral potassium, essential for regulating blood pressure and keeping muscles strong and healthy. A cup of sliced banana has nearly 600 milligrams of potassium, while a cooked plantain (since that's how most of us eat them) contains a walloping 930 milligrams. According to the National Heart, Lung, and Blood Institute at the National Institutes of Health, a high intake of potassium helps keep blood pressure in check, particularly for people who already have high blood pressure. A recent study conducted at Harvard School for Public Health found that eating just two bananas every day can dramatically lower blood pressure (it is assumed that plantains, although not part of the study, would work even better—that is, if you don't deep fry them). This is great news for millions of Americans who take ACE inhibitors to control their high blood pressure, since these medicines can have troublesome side effects. Substances in bananas cause blood vessels to widen and blood pressure to drop. Researchers say that the riper the banana, the better the effect. Another study conducted by Harvard found that the potassium power in bananas can go so far as to significantly reduce your risk of stroke.

Banana Nightcap

Bananas and plantains contain a small amount of tryptophan, an amino acid also found in milk that makes you feel relaxed and can help you get a good night's sleep. Before you go to bed, have a banana, a glass of milk, and a cookie or two—the carbohydrates in cookies help speed the tryptophan to your brain.

slightly underripe, a lot of other varieties will be far too astringent— think of unripe persimmons. But don't be discouraged if your first taste ends with a pucker; the ripe fruit is well worth the wait and even the additional price. All of these varieties—except for plantains—can be used interchangeably among the recipes in this book.

Banana Varieties

To clarify some of the terms used in the descriptions that follow, banana in general refers to a sweet "dessert" banana, like the Cavendish, which is usually eaten out of hand and in desserts. A "ladyfinger" banana is one that grows to only 4 to 6 inches in length. A "cooking" banana is somewhere between a dessert banana and a plantain, meaning it can be cooked in the same way as a plantain when it is green but will also become sweet enough to be eaten out of hand once ripe. Plantains are classified botanically a fruit but are treated like a vegetable and are almost always cooked before eating. Once ripe, the pulp can be used in a dessert, but it is usually cooked before it is incorporated into a recipe.

If you happen to be fortunate enough to live in southern Florida, you have a whole other world of bananas and plantains from which to choose, thanks to growers in that region and all the wonderful Latin food markets. If you don't live in Florida, you can occasionally find these rarer varieties in bigger cities and in some Asian markets, particularly ones specializing in Southeast Asian foods and products. Here are a few of the newer banana varieties you may come across.

Brazilian: The Brazilian banana is smaller and has an unusually sweet flavor and firm texture. Male flowers of the Brazilian banana plant are considered quite tasty. You can find banana blossoms occasionally at ethnic or specialty markets.

Burro: Although some cooking bananas are also called Burro, usually the Burro is a squat-looking dessert banana. When ripe, the skin is soft and the flesh is creamy looking. There is a slight lemony tang to its flavor. The Burro is good to snack on as well as to use in fresh-fruit desserts.

French Horn: This is a graceful, elongated plantain that is quite large, and it is fairly rare in the marketplace. Also known as the Dominica, it is a staple in South America and is often seen in the Caribbean islands as well.

Golden Aromatic, or Go San Heong: In Chinese, this name means "you can smell it from over the next mountain," and its fragrance is considered quite pleasant. In addition to being aromatic, its pulp is creamy and very sweet tasting. It resembles the Cavendish but is sweeter and has an overall superior flavor. It's one of the rarer varieties—you'd have better luck finding it in the Miami area.

Gros Michelle: This was one of the first varieties originally imported to North America but it has since been replaced by the more disease-resistant Cavendish. It is still considered one of the most delicious bananas; it is superior in flavor to the Cavendish and remains the favorite of Europeans and anyone else lucky enough to find it. Due to its susceptibility to Panama Disease and the fact that the tree is very tall and tends to blow over in tropical storms, most growers have abandoned the variety, so the fruit is hard to come by.

Hua Moa: This is a plump cooking banana that, once ripe, can be used in desserts. It has gained popularity with Miami's Cuban community, where it is widely used as a frying banana when green (it doesn't hold up well when it's ripe). When shopping in one of Miami's Latin markets, ask for a "Hawaiiano."

able to anyone who needed it. Highly effective new vaccines today cost between $50 and $100 per dose, but if the vaccine were engineered into a banana it would cost only pennies.

Other research on banana-borne vaccines involves the sexually transmitted human papilloma virus (HPV), which causes more than 200,000 deaths per year—it's the leading cause of cervical cancer in women. Other work involves generating a banana plant that would produce a protein from the hepatitis B virus.

Ice Cream: The unripe fruit has a frosty white, green exterior that turns light yellow when ripe. The flesh of the Ice Cream banana is snow white and slightly tangy. It adds a bright flavor to salads, sorbets, and smoothies.

Manzano: This is also called the Apple banana (*manzano* is the Spanish word for apple). It is short and stubby, and its flesh has an aftertaste similar to apples. It is particularly good in salad and fresh-fruit dessert recipes calling for uncooked bananas. When ripe, its skin is yellow and has a slight give to it. Manzano bananas, however, seem to have a very short shelf life.

Mysore: This is an up-and-coming ladyfinger banana from India. It is similar to the Manzano in length but is not quite as plump. It is not only a wonderful banana to eat out of hand, but has the longest shelf life of all the bananas currently available, usually lasting about ten to twelve days if not kept too warm.

Namwa: Also called Klue Namwa, this banana comes from Southeast Asia. Namwa is similar to an Ice Cream banana in that it has the same dusty white or frosty appearance in the green state, but it is sweeter and firmer. It can sometimes be found in Southeast Asian or Indian markets.

Niño: Only 3 inches long, this native of Ecuador is often called a Baby or Finger banana, and it has become a great commercial success in just the last few years. It's one of my favorites, and fortunately it can be found in most large supermarkets. The Niño is best when the skin is just yellow or slightly freckled. The flesh holds up well when cooked and maintains its creamy, rich banana flavor. It is the best possible banana to sauté, deep fry for fritters, or use in other cooked dessert recipes.

Praying Hands: This banana from Indonesia got its name because the fingers of each hand are fused together in a way that makes them look like praying hands. When ripe, they turn yellow and you can carefully pull the bananas apart with your fingers, or cut the entire hand crosswise and pry the sweet fruit from the skin with a small spoon. They have a vanilla custard–like flavor and a longer-than-normal shelf life. Praying Hands are very hard to find. If you spy a bunch, be sure and grab it before someone else does.

Red: The Red banana is the banana that's slowest to grow, mature, and ripen. It is grown throughout the tropics and is often called Jamaican Red, Cuban Red, Hawaiian Red, or in Costa Rica, Macaboo. I've seen both stubby and plump or small and slender Red bananas at my local supermarket (like the Niño, the Red is more widely available now). It takes a little longer to ripen, but once ripe, keeps very well. I have had Red bananas sitting at room temperature for nearly two weeks, and they were still delicious. The taste of the peach-colored flesh may remind you of a cross between raspberries and peaches. Like the Niño, it holds up well when cooked. Its strong banana flavor makes it perfect for smoothies, sorbets, pies, puddings, and cakes.

Cooking with Bananas

For the best results when using bananas in a recipe, make sure that you use fruit at the proper stage of ripeness. For instance, to get the most banana flavor when you bake with bananas you want ripe, but not overripe, fruit. Bananas that have a lot of spots and are totally brown (even with a few fruit flies flying around) are what is meant by "very ripe" in the recipes. If the flesh seems watery and has a fermented odor when you remove the peel, the banana is overripe and

*S*tores, mail-order catalogs, and even produce departments feature hooks, hangers, and ripening bowls designed to hold and protect bananas from bruising while they ripen. Do they work? Good Housekeeping Institute recently tested six ripening methods to see what worked best. They placed several bunches of green bananas on a hanger, on a plastic hook in a cabinet, in a dome-covered bowl with breathing holes, in brown paper bags, and in a regular bowl placed on a kitchen counter. The results? After five days all the bananas were fully ripe except those on the hanger. So simply placing your fruit in a bowl is still top banana, unless you want to extend the life of your bunch, in which case get a hanger.

past its prime. If you want to hold on to your bananas and prevent them from further ripening, you can refrigerate them, but only for a few days. (Do not refrigerate green bananas—the cold will interrupt the ripening process.) Also, be sure to keep your other refrigerated fruits and vegetables away from the bananas as the ethylene gas the bananas emit will affect their flavor and freshness.

Banana purée is used in many of the recipes in this book. Since bananas can vary in size and their yield tends to shrink as they ripen, many of the baking recipes call for cup measurements of purée. (For small amounts you may also want to try varieties that are smaller than standard bananas.) In the recipes I have given both the measurement and the number of bananas required, but here are some guidelines:

1 medium banana = about ⅓ cup purée
1¼ bananas = about ½ cup purée
3 medium bananas = about 1 cup purée

You can freeze ripe-banana purée by mixing in a tablespoon of lemon juice per cup and placing small amounts of purée in plastic freezer containers (measure the banana purée before freezing it and label accordingly).

To freeze whole fruit, peel the ripe banana and wrap it tightly in plastic wrap to keep out any air. Frozen whole bananas will keep for several weeks. If you plan on using the bananas within a few days, peel a few at a time and place them in a self-sealing freezer bag—they may stick together, but they come apart fairly easily.

For savory dishes, a less sweet flavor is usually desired. Choose bananas that still have a little green on the tips or ones that have just turned fully yellow with no spots (unless the recipe specifies green bananas, in which case you'll want to use the greenest you can find).

For dessert recipes that call for sautéing or cooking bananas, use bananas that are just ripe so that they will hold up better in the recipe

*W*hen it comes to ripening plantains, I put them in a brown paper bag since I think it helps the process along (or maybe it just makes me feel better). Turn the plantains every few days so that they will ripen on both sides evenly. Keep them away from direct sources of heat and sunlight, however, as this may dehydrate them or "cook" them before you get a chance to.

and not turn into mush. For fresh-fruit recipes, sprinkle the bananas or brush them lightly with lemon, lime, orange, or pineapple juice to keep them from turning brown.

Plantains and Green Bananas

Plantains are usually much larger than bananas and are long and angular—some people think of them as simply ugly bananas. The plantain is a fruit but is often referred to as the vegetable banana for its use as a starchy side dish. You'll find several types of plantains in markets, among them Giant or Puerto Rican Dwarf Plantains, the latter of which can be quite fat and plump with a creamy texture. Some can weigh as much as a pound each. You can usually find them in large supermarkets or in Latin or Asian markets and produce stands (they're also available through mail order—see Sources, page 182). The plantain may be banana's ugly cousin, but inside, its peachy flesh has a flavor that changes dramatically as it ripens. Hard, green plantains are used in a variety of dishes, usually fried; in this stage, the plantain has a taste and texture similar to a potato. Semiripe plantains are usually yellow and slightly soft to the touch. Ripe means the skin is completely black and there are even a few fruit flies hovering about. Semiripe and ripe plantains have more sugar, and they taste similar to a winter variety squash or sweet potato.

It's often difficult to find ripe plantains, so if you want to cook with them, you'll need to plan ahead. They can take a long time to reach an ideal, soft, ripe stage—perhaps even two to three weeks—so it's best to buy many at a time so you can use greener ones for certain recipes while setting some aside to ripen for other uses. Sometimes due to improper storage (usually refrigeration at too-low temperatures for too long), the plantains you buy never ripen but simply turn hard, dry up, and become petrified. This happened a lot to me when I

*G*reen and semiripe plantains and green bananas are not as easy to peel as ripe fruit. To do so, first cut the ends off, then cut the fruit in half crosswise. Using a sharp paring knife, cut a shallow slit down the inner curve of the banana or plantain. Use your fingers to pry off the skin.

began cooking plantains, until I found another store that seemed to know that it's best not to refrigerate them. If this happens to you, just throw them on the compost heap and try again.

Sometimes it's hard to find plantains at all in some areas, so for most of the recipes in this book, standard green bananas can be substituted—at this stage they are mostly starch and are similar in texture to plantains. You'll just need to use a few more to make up for the size difference. If you don't see green fruit in the banana display, ask the produce manager if there are some in the back—usually the answer is yes.

Banana Leaves

The leaf of the banana plant has many uses in different cultures. Some varieties of bananas are grown specifically for the leaves, which can be woven into a rope or basket, used as an umbrella or as a roof for a home, or as a plate or serving platter. More often, though, it is used as a wrap for cooking all types of foods (since aluminum foil is not exactly a commodity in rain forests).

Perhaps the largest wrap of all is for kalua pig, the Hawaiian pork barbecue, which is similar to a clam bake. A large pit is dug and lined with stones. A wood fire heats the stones and creates hot coals. Fresh banana leaves are cut and placed over the coals to make a steam bed for a whole pig. Sweet potatoes and such are placed around the pig to fill in gaps, then another layer of leaves goes on top, along with more rocks to weigh down the leaves, creating a sort of cooking cocoon. Some hours later the pig is unearthed for the feast.

Banana leaves smell sweet when cooking, and they lend a delicate flavor and fragrance to food that is steamed, grilled, or boiled in them. It is customary to serve the food in the leaf it is cooked in, though the leaf itself is never eaten.

"Pa-chiao has leaves as large as mats. One stem bears several tens of fruits. The fruit has a reddish skin the color of fire, and when peeled the inside is dark. The pulp is edible and very sweet, like honey or sugar. Four or five of these fruits are enough for a meal. After eating, the flavor lingers on among the teeth."

—Chinese scholar Yang Fu, written in the second century A.D. in a compilation titled Record of Strange Things

You can sometimes find fresh leaves, but I have seen them only rarely in ethnic markets in New York (if you live in Miami or Hawaii, then rejoice). You can also buy fresh leaves via mail order (see Sources, page 182). But frozen leaves, usually in one-pound packages, are inexpensive and can be found in most Latin and Asian specialty markets year round. To use them, soak the folded stack of frozen leaves in warm water until thawed and pliable. (You'll need to pour boiling water over fresh leaves to make them pliable.) Gently unfold the leaves and cut them with scissors to the required size. Use damp paper towels to wipe the leaves, which often have a white film on them, working in the direction of the veins to avoid tearing. Unused leaves can be refolded, wrapped in plastic wrap, and frozen again for future use.

Banana Blossoms

Unless you live in an area where there are banana groves or near a large Asian supermarket, it can be extremely difficult to find banana blossoms. They are large, reddish-purple, cone-shaped pods the size of small cabbages. I have seen them fresh and frozen once, only to never see them again. Again, if you live near Miami or Hawaii (or grow your own) your chances are better. Cooked blossoms can be slightly bitter, a bit like endive or escarole and for some, maybe an acquired taste. (I'm a bit wild about them.) You must first peel the blossom, artichoke fashion, down to its tender center. Then you need to boil it first in salted water before using it in a recipe. I've included one recipe for a wonderful Banana Blossom Salad (page 52). It makes an exotic addition to any Asian-flavored meal.

A Slice of Banana History

Bananas have an ancient history. The ancestor of the perky yellow fruit we buy at the supermarket was tough and seedy with only a modicum of pulp. Most experts believe these early bananas came about many thousands of years ago in the rain forests of Southeast Asia. Wild varieties of bananas can still be found there. It took many more years for the banana to evolve into the plump, mostly seedless fruit of today. These experts point to the wisdom (not to mention hunger), of early humans who, sensing the immense value of the fruit, cultivated those plants that mutated and produced fruits with few seeds and more pulp. These early farmers probably recognized the sweetness of the banana as a signal that the fruit was not only okay to eat but—like berries and even grains—was also a food that could sustain a body through famine.

Botanically speaking, the banana (and plantain) is a member of the genus *Musa*, which is part of a much larger family of plants that includes ginger, lilies, orchids, palms, arrowroots, canes, and various tropical grasses. Though most people think that bananas grow on trees, the banana plant is actually the world's largest herb, and the fruit is its berry.

A Romantic Past

There are many legends surrounding the banana in the world's cultures. The Hindus were probably the first to immortalize the banana under the name of *tala* or *pala* throughout the sacred books of ancient India. You can see banana leaves sculpted into ancient Buddhist works of art, and in Bengal it is still considered good luck to be married beneath the leaves of a banana plant.

The banana also holds an esteemed position in the Koran, where it is the original Tree of Paradise and the fruit God forbade Adam and Eve to taste. After the "great transgression," they covered their nakedness not with fig leaves but with the much more ample leaves of the banana plant. A variation of this legend also shows up in medieval Europe and the story may have trickled down through the ages, for the French and Italian terms for the fruit are *figue d'Adam* and *fico d'Adamo*, respectively.

According to Hawaiian legend, plantains were brought to the islands by the brother of the volcano goddess, Pele. Because of its phallic shape, the plantain (or banana) became *kapu*, which means it could only be eaten by men. If a woman so much as touched a banana stalk, it meant certain death.

Most experts agree that Westerner's first recorded taste of the banana occurred in 327 B.C. According to the Roman naturalist Pliny the Elder (23–79 A.D.), members of Alexander the Great's expedition to India were most impressed with the fruit. Pliny told of the encounter in his *Historia Naturalis:* "There is [a] tree of India . . . remarkable for the size and sweetness of its fruit, upon which the sages of India live," he wrote. "The leaf of this tree resembles in shape the wing of a bird. . . . It puts forth its fruit from the bark . . . a single one containing sufficient to satisfy four persons. This tree is called *pala* and its fruit, *ariena.*"

Many theories exist about the spread of the banana from Asia to the Western world during ancient times, but most bananologists credit Arab merchants with introducing the plant to Africa and the Middle East. By the time Portuguese explorers of the mid-fifteenth century reached the Guinea Coast, they found the banana and the plantain to be a well-established staple of the African diet. It is from the Portuguese interpretation of the multiple West African names for the fruit—*banna, bana, gbana, funana, abana,* and *banane*—that the derivation of the word "banana" eventually came about. And it was also the Portuguese who took the banana to the Canary Islands and eventually the larger islands of the Caribbean.

In 1516 a Spanish friar, Tomás de Berlanga (who later became Bishop of Panama), sailed from the Canaries to what is now South America. Along with his bibles he brought banana plants—as well as oranges and lemons—to the New World. They were planted first on the island of Hispaniola, where they grew and multiplied from Mexico to Paraguay and points beyond. Five centuries earlier, Polynesians had taken banana plants eastward from Asia to the islands of the South Pacific, and so, finally, the banana had managed to circumnavigate the globe. By the seventeenth century the existence of the fruit throughout South America is heavily documented.

Not too many years after bananas were transplanted to the New World, the fruit showed up in Tudor England. A recent discovery by archeologists from the Museum of London, who were digging in a 400-year-old trash dump, unearthed a nearly intact, six-inch-long banana peel thought to be from the sixteenth century. It is the oldest banana peel ever found. It was an important discovery as it was previously thought that bananas did not arrive on English soil until some 150 years later. Researchers working on the project speculated that the fruit may have come to London from Africa as a result of trade with Spain and Portugal.

For Americans, it was not exactly love at first bite when it came to bananas. One account has it that some Caribbean-grown fruit—

perhaps of questionable condition—made it to American shores in 1690 to Salem, Massachusetts. Puritans boiled the bananas (or plantains, we don't know which) with pork and did not like the results, saying that the fruit tasted like "soap." There may have been occasions in the following decades when a sea captain would manage to get a few bunches to dry land before they succumbed to mold and rot (ships regularly traveled from Caribbean ports to colonial ones before the Revolutionary War). The first legitimate account appears in 1804, when a schooner named *Reynard* allegedly brought thirty bunches from Cuba to New York. More significantly, in 1843, a New York dealer named John Pearsall is reported to have brought in and auctioned three hundred bunches of the russet-colored "Cuban Reds." The price was twenty-five cents a finger, an exorbitant amount at the time.

Whenever bananas did make it into port cities, they sold at very high prices, and there were merchants eager to meet the demand. The irony was that bananas are the rabbits of the plant world, constantly bearing fruit year-round, so there were great profits to be made. But bananas were—and still are for that matter—highly perishable and lasted only a few weeks once the stem of the fruit was cut from the plant. The lengthy sea voyages prevented the fruit from becoming a commodity in the United States until the late-nineteenth century.

The banana remained a rare and expensive delicacy for the well-to-do throughout the eighteenth and most of the nineteenth centuries. (Early etiquette books instructed the diner to first peel the fruit, lay it on a dessert plate, and to slice and eat it with a fruit knife and fork). America's great love affair with the banana really began at its birthday party in Philadelphia in 1876. This was the Centennial Exposition, something of a world's fair and celebratory ball that was attended by thousands of citizens and some token foreign royalty. Some of the century's greatest curiosities and inventions were put on found with the lowest levels of pesticides, according to a recent report issued by Consumer's Union. The consumer's advocacy group analyzed the most recent data collected by the U.S. Department of Agriculture and created a toxicity index that ranked foods according to the frequency of pesticide detection, the levels of residues present, and the relative toxicity of the detected residues. There were only six foods that earned relatively "clean" marks based on the index: frozen or canned corn, milk, U.S.-made orange juice, U.S.-grown broccoli, canned peaches and bananas.

display, including the typewriter, the telephone, the refrigerator, and among an array of specimens in the agricultural exhibition, a sad-looking tropical plant called the banana. Bananas were gaily wrapped in colored tinfoil and sold for ten cents a piece—a high price at the time—and crowds waited in line to purchase them, even though most of the bananas were well past their prime. This, however, did not prevent the banana from becoming a sensation, and consumer demand created a hot market for importers.

Although import firms were proliferating, many banana importers started up only to be forced into bankruptcy when a hurricane either devastated a plantation or prevented a ship from reaching port before the shipment turned to mush. But enough of them persevered to forge what would later become an empire.

It was the United Fruit Company (predecessor of Chiquita), that first achieved a constant, year-round flow of bananas from Latin America to the North American market. (Its multifarious role in Central America's economy and political situations gave rise to the term "banana republic.") In doing so, it transformed the fruit overnight from a luxury item affordable only to a few to a household staple. In 1903, the same year that it was listed on the New York Stock Exchange, the United Fruit Company revolutionized ocean transport by launching the world's first refrigerated produce boat, the SS *Venus*. Just two years later in 1905, the company imported a record three and a half billion bananas. That meant the consumption rate in the United States would have been forty bananas per person a year.

Today that figure has doubled. According to the Produce Marketing Association, each American consumes more than twenty-eight pounds of bananas a year—that's around eighty medium bananas. About 65 percent of all American households buy bananas every week, which makes bananas the most popular fresh fruit by far (we eat about nineteen pounds of apples a year, followed by watermelon at seventeen pounds).

How Bananas Grow

Organic Bananas

*O*rganic banana farms are a fast-growing industry. Like conventional banana growers, organic farmers use chemicals that protect against insects and disease, but these are nonsynthetic, "biological" materials that are considered less toxic to workers and consumers. In lieu of herbicides, more machete-wielding farm workers are dispatched to deal with clearing weeds and vegetation. This is probably the biggest reason organic bananas cost more—sometimes double the price—than conventionally grown bananas.

Banana plants thrive where conditions are both hot and humid— the tropics and subtropics of Central and South America, Africa, the Caribbean, the South Pacific, Asia, and Southeast Asia. The primary banana-exporting countries are Ecuador, Costa Rica, Panama, Honduras, Colombia, Guatemala, and the Philippines. Bananas from African and Caribbean countries supply most of Europe with fruit. The Cavendish variety is the one most commonly grown for export. The plant is one of the shorter varieties, so it's less vulnerable to windstorms; it is also fairly disease resistant.

Banana plants require a fairly constant temperature of 80°F and rainfall of about four inches per month to produce consistent crops. With the right amount of sunlight, water, and drainage, they grow quite fast—from fifteen to thirty feet in a single year. Banana plants can grow well for home gardeners in the South where the climate is more tropical. Banana plants can be grown in temperate climates during the summer, but most varieties will not tolerate cooler temperatures and must be dug up and brought indoors wherever the ground freezes solid. It is very difficult for these short-season banana plants to produce fruit.

Banana plants are grown from a sucker or rhizome. Suckers are the small banana plants that spring up at the base of the mother plant. Banana farmers cut down most of the mother plants with a machete, leaving the strongest suckers—or "daughters"—to grow into new plants. The rhizome is a fat, bulblike root. Like a potato, it has eyes that can be cut and transplanted to form new plants.

Since the banana plant is not a tree, it does not have a true trunk; rather, its trunk is formed by overlapping leaves—similar to a giant celery stalk—that create a large sheathlike base. Although the banana stalk is more than 90 percent water, it is strong enough to support what is called the "true stem" that grows when the plant reaches ma-

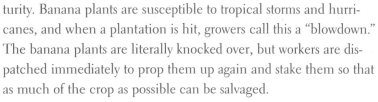

turity. Banana plants are susceptible to tropical storms and hurricanes, and when a plantation is hit, growers call this a "blowdown." The banana plants are literally knocked over, but workers are dispatched immediately to prop them up again and stake them so that as much of the crop as possible can be salvaged.

After eight or nine months, a banana plant sprouts a vividly colored bud from the center of a leaf cluster. Growing ever larger, it will eventually produce flowers attached to small tubes called ovaries. These will develop from six to fifteen clusters called "hands." Each hand contains ten to twenty bananas, or "fingers." A single plant can produce a bunch weighing more than a hundred pounds. It takes about two to three months for a bunch of bananas to mature. If properly maintained, banana plants can bear fruit about every ten months. The average crop yields per acre for banana plantations is enormous—about seven tons annually.

Though banana yields are great, the profit margin for bananas is not, so the plant is handled with great care and delicacy. Workers are constantly clearing away jungle growth, propping the plant with poles to support its heavy stem as it bends from the weight of its growing fruit, and irrigating the fields during dry seasons. Developing fruit is wrapped in plastic to protect it against the sun, wind, birds, and insects. Unlike many other fruits, bananas ripen best off the plant and are cut while still green (in other words, it's not just for the convenience of growers). If left to ripen on the plant—there are a few exceptions depending on the banana variety—the fruit develops a mealy texture and less sweet taste, and it is likely to burst and rot. The distance a banana must travel determines the day on which it is picked, for days and even hours matter in its fragile life.

It takes two workers to harvest bananas from a plant. A "cutter" will cut the plant down with a machete and the "backer" waits in anticipation for the stem to settle on his shoulder. The cutter then cuts the stem, and the backer takes it to a nearby overhead cable that carries

the fruit to a processing plant. Once the banana plant produces its bunch of bananas, its life is over and the plant is cut away, leaving a side-shoot successor to take its place.

Before being packed into special cardboard boxes holding forty pounds of bananas, the bananas are removed from the stem, separated into hands, then clusters, washed in large water tanks, and sorted and graded. It normally takes from two to two and half weeks for the bananas to go from harvest to a supermarket shelf. After packing, the boxes are loaded onto refrigerated ships that hold from 150,000 to 200,000 boxes. The babying process continues on the boat, where the fruit is cooled to a carefully maintained 58°F to retard the ripening process that began in the field, and to draw out the field heat. This is important since a banana begins to generate heat for the ripening process as soon as it is picked. Internal fruit temperatures are taken hourly during the voyage. (This is critical: last year a malfunctioning refrigeration unit on a $1.4 million boatload of Del Monte bananas turned the multi-ton shipment into banana sludge.) The boat trip can take from three days to a week depending on the country of origin and the port of entry in the United States.

The fruit is then distributed to wholesalers, fruit-ripening specialists known as "ripeners," and to supermarket warehouses. At this point the bananas are still very green, so they are placed in ripening rooms, which are large-capacity refrigerated and ventilated holding rooms. Bananas are ripened commercially similar to the way that they are stored on the ship. Temperature and humidity levels are controlled, and the air is circulated as the temperature of the fruit is gently raised by degrees. Ethylene gas stimulates the ripening process in bananas (as well as other fruits such as tomatoes, apples, and pineapples). Additional, synthetic ethylene is added to assist in the ripening process and to ripen the bananas to the degree desired by the produce buyer. Bananas are not brought to the actual eating stage of ripeness

because it would limit their shelf life; instead, they are brought to a color state called No. 4 in the trade, in which yellow begins to show through the bright green shade of the field bananas. A fully ripe, yellow and lightly spotted banana is a No. 7, the stage of ripeness that most people prefer.

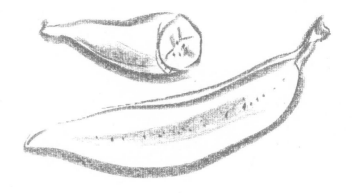

Bananas for *Breakfast*

Memorable Moment from Woody Allen's film Bananas

Fielding Mellish: You're busy tonight?

Norma: Some old friends are coming over. We're gonna show some pornographic movies.

Fielding Mellish: You need an usher?

Sour Cream–Banana Pancakes with Nutmeg Syrup

I once had banana pancakes with nutmeg syrup when I was visiting a spice plantation on the island of Grenada, where nutmeg is used in and on just about everything. I couldn't stop thinking about the pancakes and so came up with this version. If you love nutmeg as much as I do, you'll want to grate a bit more over the pancakes when you add the butter and maple syrup.

Makes 4 servings

1 cup all-purpose flour

2 teaspoons baking powder

1/2 teaspoon salt

1/4 teaspoon baking soda

1/4 teaspoon freshly grated nutmeg

2 ripe bananas, finely diced

1 tablespoon brown sugar

1 large egg

1/2 cup sour cream

1/4 cup milk

1 teaspoon pure vanilla extract

2 tablespoons butter, melted

Warm maple syrup mixed with a
    pinch of freshly grated nutmeg

Stir together the flour, baking powder, salt, baking soda, and nutmeg in a large bowl. In a medium bowl partially mash the banana with a fork. Whisk in the brown sugar, egg, sour cream, milk, vanilla, and butter. Pour the egg mixture into the flour mixture and whisk together until the flour is just moistened (do not overmix).

Heat a griddle or a large, nonstick skillet over medium heat until hot, and brush lightly with vegetable oil. Using a measuring cup, drop 1/3 cup of the batter onto the griddle, cooking a few pancakes at a time. Cook about 4 minutes on one side, or until there are bubbles on top and the edges appear dry. Turn the pancakes with a wide spatula and cook 4 to 5 minutes more, until golden brown. Transfer the pancakes to a platter in a 200°F oven to keep them warm while you cook the remaining batter, brushing the griddle with more oil as necessary.

Plantain-Pecan-Cornmeal Pancakes

Plantain combined with mace yields a pumpkiny flavor that will remind you of fall. With pecans and maple syrup, these light corn cakes make a comforting country breakfast. Serve them with sausage links and freshly squeezed orange juice. If you can't find ripe plantains, you can substitute 1½ firm-ripe bananas.

Makes 4 servings

2 tablespoons butter

1 very ripe plantain, peeled, quartered, and thinly sliced

½ cup all-purpose flour

½ cup yellow cornmeal

1 tablespoon baking powder

2 tablespoons brown sugar

½ teaspoon salt

1 cup milk

1 large egg

⅓ cup chopped pecans, toasted, plus more for garnish

Pure maple syrup, heated

Heat the butter in a medium skillet over medium heat. Cook the plantain, stirring until it turns golden and is soft. Combine the flour, cornmeal, baking powder, brown sugar, salt, milk, and egg in a blender and purée until smooth. Transfer the batter to a large measuring cup or bowl and stir in the plantains and pecans. (If the batter seems too thick, add more milk.)

Heat a griddle or large, preferably nonstick skillet over medium heat and lightly brush it with vegetable oil. Spoon about ¼ cup of the batter onto the griddle, leaving 1 or 2 inches between pancakes. Cook until bubbles appear on the top of the cakes and the bottom is golden brown. Turn pancakes and cook until the other side is golden brown. Transfer pancakes to a baking sheet in a 200°F oven to keep warm while you cook the remaining batter.

Serve pancakes hot with butter and maple syrup and garnish with chopped pecans, if desired.

Banana Oat Waffles

Beaten egg whites, folded in at the last minute, are the secret to these light, yet crisp banana waffles. Use very ripe fruit so the waffles will have a deep, banana flavor. I use a Belgian waffle iron, but if you have a different kind, follow the manufacturer's directions for the amount of batter to use per waffle grid.

Makes 4 to 6 servings

1 cup all-purpose flour

1 cup old-fashioned oats

$^1/_4$ cup packed light brown sugar

1 tablespoon baking powder

$^1/_2$ teaspoon baking soda

$^1/_4$ teaspoon salt

$^1/_2$ teaspoon ground cinnamon

$^1/_2$ teaspoon ground nutmeg

3 large eggs, separated

$1^3/_4$ cups buttermilk

4 tablespoons unsalted butter, melted

1 teaspoon pure vanilla extract

2 very ripe bananas

1 tablespoon fresh lemon juice

$^1/_2$ cup chopped pecans, toasted, optional

1 ripe banana, diced

Pure maple syrup and butter

Heat the waffle iron. In a large bowl, stir together the flour, oats, brown sugar, baking powder, baking soda, salt, cinnamon, and nutmeg. In another bowl, whisk together the egg yolks, buttermilk, butter, and vanilla. Mash the bananas with the lemon juice and add to the bowl with the buttermilk. Whip the egg whites until stiff but not dry. Pour the buttermilk mixture into the dry ingredients and stir until just blended. Fold in the egg whites and the nuts, if using.

Ladle about $^1/_3$ cup of the batter into each section of the waffle grid and use a wooden spoon to spread the batter almost to the edges. Close the lid and bake 5 to 6 minutes, or until no more steam emerges from the waffle iron. Transfer cooked waffles to a baking sheet and keep warm in a 200°F oven. Repeat with remaining batter, spraying waffle grids with vegetable oil in between batches, if necessary.

To serve, heat the diced banana with maple syrup and butter and pour over the waffles.

Banana Crepes with Strawberry Maple Syrup

I can't make crepes without thinking of my friend Peri Aronian, who is the innkeeper, gardener, and head chef at her own little bed and breakfast in Montauk, New York. One Sunday morning I wandered into Peri's warm kitchen to find her simultaneously grinding coffee beans and cooking her perfect crepes. Hers are a model of what every crepe should be: thin, light, and golden brown. On this morning, she sautéed sliced bananas in a little butter, folded them up in the crepes, and drizzled on strawberry-maple syrup. With freshly brewed coffee and orange juice, crepes are ideal for brunch. But they're also terrific for dessert: just top the banana crepes with vanilla ice cream. Before inviting guests over, I advise practicing your technique. You won't have any trouble getting rid of your trial batches: they'll keep up to three days, wrapped in plastic wrap and refrigerated (longer if frozen). Warm each one briefly in a hot pan before filling.

Makes 4 to 6 servings

12 warm 8- to 9-inch crepes
  (recipe below)
1¹/₂ tablespoons butter
6 firm-ripe bananas, cut in
  half lengthwise

³/₄ cup pure maple syrup
Pinch of ground cinnamon
1¹/₂ tablespoons strawberry jam
  or preserves
Confectioners' sugar for dusting

In a large, preferably nonstick skillet, melt the butter over medium heat. Arrange the bananas, cut side down, in the pan. Cook them (in batches, if necessary) about 10 minutes, or until they are glazed and slightly softened, but not mushy.

Warm the maple syrup in a small pan over low heat. Stir in the cinnamon and strawberry jam, and heat until dissolved.

Place one crepe on a plate and top with a banana half. Loosely fold or roll the crepe around the banana. Drizzle with syrup. Repeat with remaining crepes and bananas, figuring 2 to 3 crepes per person. Lightly dust the crepes with confectioners' sugar before serving with more syrup on the side.

Basic Crepes

Makes twelve to sixteen 8- or 9-inch crepes

1 cup all-purpose flour

$^1/_4$ teaspoon salt

2 large eggs

1$^1/_4$ cups milk

2 tablespoons butter, melted and cooled

In a blender or large bowl of a food processor, combine the flour, salt, eggs, milk, and melted butter. Pulse five times. Remove the lid and scrape down the sides. Pulse five more times, or until the ingredients are well blended. Pour the batter into a bowl or large measuring cup. Cover and refrigerate 15 to 30 minutes. The batter should be the consistency of half-and-half. If necessary, whisk in a little more flour or milk to make it the correct consistency. Stir the batter well before using.

Lightly brush a 9- or 10-inch crepe pan or nonstick skillet with butter and place it over medium heat. When the pan is hot, but not smoking, remove it from the heat with one hand; pour in a little less than $^1/_4$ cup batter with the other. Immediately shake, tilt, and turn the pan so that the batter runs from side to side and covers the entire bottom.

Return the pan to the heat and loosen the edges of the crepe with a spatula. Cook 1 minute, or until the top of the crepe looks dry and the bottom is evenly browned. Turn with a spatula and brown the other side, about 20 to 30 seconds. Place the crepe on a plate lined with a sheet of wax paper (place the golden brown "good" side of the crepe down so that when you roll it up, this will be on the outside). Continue making crepes, brushing the pan lightly with butter after each crepe and stacking the finished crepes as you go. Crepes can be made up to three days ahead—just cover them tightly with plastic wrap and refrigerate. Briefly warm each crepe in a hot pan before using.

Bananas for Breakfast

Banana-Stuffed French Toast

The soft, warm banana hidden inside this orange-flavored French toast is a delightful surprise. This is a fairly rich version that you might want to consider serving for dessert with a dab of crème fraîche or sour cream.

Makes 4 servings

2 firm-ripe bananas

4 eggs

$^3/_4$ cup half-and-half

$^3/_4$ cup milk

3 tablespoons Cointreau or
   Grand Marnier

Grated zest of 1 orange

$^1/_2$ teaspoon cinnamon

1 tablespoon brown sugar

Pinch of salt

1 large loaf of challah, brioche, or
   Italian bread

2 tablespoons butter

Confectioners' sugar for dusting

Maple syrup

Cut the bananas into ¼-inch-thick diagonal slices. Whisk together the eggs, half-and-half, milk, liqueur, orange zest, cinnamon, brown sugar, and salt. Set aside.

Slice off the heels of the bread and discard. Cut the loaf into eight 1-inch pieces. Then cut bread slices horizontally nearly in half, leaving one edge intact to create a pocket. Fill each bread pocket with 4 or more banana slices. Place the stuffed bread in a large, deep baking dish in one layer. Pour the egg mixture over them, and allow to soak 5 minutes on each side, until all liquid is absorbed.

Heat the butter in a large, nonstick skillet over medium heat. Cook the toast in batches (adding more butter, if necessary), about 5 to 6 minutes per side, until golden brown. Transfer the cooked slices to a baking sheet in a warm (250°F) oven. Place 2 pieces of toast on a plate, dust with confectioners' sugar, and serve with warm maple syrup.

Banana Toast

A yummy, easy, and very kid-friendly breakfast. If desired, top the toast with crisp bacon slices or cooked ham before adding the banana or plantain slices. You can also skip the sugar topping and spread the toast with your favorite jam.

Makes 2 servings

1¹/2 firm-ripe bananas, or ripe, black-skinned plantains

2 tablespoons butter

2 large slices sourdough or Italian bread, lightly toasted

1 teaspoon brown sugar mixed with a pinch of nutmeg

Peel the banana or plantain and cut into long, diagonal slices, about $\frac{1}{3}$-inch thick. Heat the butter in a large skillet, and cook the banana slices over medium heat about 1 minute per side (a minute or two longer for the plantain), until just soft. Butter the toast and arrange banana slices on top. Sprinkle the brown sugar mixture over the top and serve warm.

Strawberry-Banana Bruschetta

This deluxe version of cinnamon toast tastes both fresh and fruity, and is a little decadent with the sour cream and bubbling brown sugar on top. It's a nice quick breakfast you can make in the toaster oven, or serve it with an egg dish for brunch.

Makes 4 servings

Half a French baguette, cut into
  $^3/_4$-inch slices, lightly toasted
1$^1/_2$ tablespoons butter, melted
2 tablespoons granulated sugar
$^1/_2$ teaspoon ground cinnamon
$^1/_2$ cup diced nectarine

$^1/_4$ cup diced strawberries
1 firm-ripe banana, diced
1 tablespoon lemon juice
$^1/_4$ cup sour cream or yogurt
Brown sugar for sprinkling
Mint sprigs, optional

Preheat the oven to 375°F. Lightly brush toasted bread on one side with butter. Stir together 1 tablespoon of the granulated sugar with the cinnamon and sprinkle evenly over the bread slices. Place toast on a large baking sheet and bake 5 minutes, or until the tops are toasted and crusty.

Toss the nectarine, strawberries, and banana with the remaining tablespoon of sugar and the lemon juice. Spoon the fruit mixture on the toast and top with a dollop of sour cream. Sprinkle the tops with brown sugar, and place the baking sheet under a preheated broiler about 1 minute, or until tops are bubbling. Serve immediately and garnish with mint sprigs, if desired.

Fufu

Fufu, also known as foofoo, foufou, or putu, is a starchy side dish of African origin that is also made from yams, cassava, corn, or rice. It's usually rather plain and is shaped into balls and often dipped into stews or similarly used to soak up rich meat juices. Here is another variation with plantains, but instead of rolling the fufu into balls, the mixture is pressed into a skillet and baked like a frittata. It has a soft consistency and makes a nice brunch dish with poached eggs.

Makes 4 to 6 servings

2 green plantains

1 tablespoon vegetable oil

2 garlic cloves, minced

1 small onion, finely chopped

$^{1}/_{2}$ pound ground pork or mild sausage

1 teaspoon red pepper flakes, optional

1 teaspoon salt

$^{1}/_{4}$ teaspoon freshly milled black pepper

Bring a large pot of water to a boil. Cut the plantains crosswise, skins on, into 2-inch pieces. Add to the boiling water and cook until the plantains are soft, about 25 minutes.

While the plantains are boiling, heat the oil in a 10-inch heavy-bottomed skillet and cook the garlic and onion until soft. Add the pork and pepper flakes, if using, and cook until it is almost done but still a little pink. Set aside.

Drain the plantains, reserving $^{1}/_{2}$ cup water. Remove the skins and mash the plantains with a potato masher (or purée in a food processor), adding a little of the cooking water to make it smooth and easier to work. Mix the plantains and pork together and add the salt and pepper. Return the mixture to the skillet and cook on medium-low heat about 20 minutes, or until the bottom is lightly browned. Cut the fufu into wedges and serve hot.

Blueberry-Banana Coffee Cake

A large cappuccino, a warm slice of this scrumptious coffee cake, and the Sunday newspaper is an ideal weekend breakfast.

Makes 6 to 8 servings

Topping:

$1/2$ **cup slivered almonds, toasted**

4 tablespoons unsalted butter, cold

$1/2$ **cup all-purpose flour**

$1/2$ **cup packed light-brown sugar**

$1/2$ **teaspoon ground cinnamon**

$1^1/2$ **cups blueberries, rinsed and picked over**

Cake:

$1/2$ **cup unsalted butter, softened**

$1/2$ **cup granulated sugar**

1 large egg

$1/2$ **teaspoon pure almond extract**

1 ripe banana, diced

$1/2$ **cup sour cream, at room temperature**

2 teaspoons finely grated lemon zest

$1^1/2$ **cups all-purpose flour**

2 teaspoons baking powder

$1/2$ **teaspoon baking soda**

$1/2$ **teaspoon salt**

Preheat the oven to 375°F. Butter a 10-inch pie plate or a 9-inch-square baking pan.

To make the topping: Place the almonds, butter, flour, brown sugar, and cinnamon in the bowl of a food processor and pulse a few times to combine. Toss the almond mixture with the blueberries in a bowl and refrigerate while you make the cake batter.

To make the cake: Cream the butter, sugar, egg, and almond extract in a large bowl with an electric mixer until light. Beat in the banana, sour cream, and lemon zest. Stir together the flour, baking powder, baking soda, and salt and gradually add to the butter mixture, mixing on low until just incorporated (the mixture will be very thick, almost like biscuit dough). Scrape the batter into the prepared pan and spread it to the edges evenly. Scatter the topping over the top of the batter. Bake 45 to 50 minutes, until the cake seems firm in the center and the edges are brown and pull away from the sides of the pan. Place on a rack to cool completely.

Plantain Tortilla

This is rather like a frittata and is a nice fast breakfast or late-night dinner. To make it a more substantial meal, add some crumbled crisp bacon or sausage.

Makes 4 to 6 servings

2 tablespoons olive oil

1 garlic clove, minced

1 large onion, thinly sliced

1 red bell pepper, thinly sliced

1 ripe, black-skinned plantain

6 large eggs

2 tablespoons minced fresh cilantro
or parsley

$1/2$ cup grated Parmesan cheese

Salt

Freshly milled black pepper

Heat the oil in a medium skillet, preferably nonstick. Sauté the garlic, onion, and pepper over medium heat until soft. Set aside. Peel and dice the plantain and boil in salted water for 5 minutes until soft; drain.

Preheat the oven to 350°F. Beat together the eggs with a whisk and add the cilantro, Parmesan, and salt and pepper to taste. Stir in the sautéed vegetables and the plantain. Return to the skillet and place over medium-low heat. Cook without stirring for 10 minutes, or until the bottom is lightly browned. Place in the oven and bake 10 to 15 minutes longer, or until the eggs on top are no longer runny. Cool for 2 minutes, then cut into wedges and serve while hot.

Bananas for Breakfast

Banana-Peach Breakfast Yogurt

I had my first taste of fresh yogurt and homemade muesli in a quaint little hotel in Venice. The clever cook had added grated bananas and berries to the bowl, and the creamy mixture was perfect breakfast food. The memory of that stay comes back to me whenever I make a bowl of this. Grating banana with a box grater over your cereal may seem a bit tedious, but you get more banana flavor per bite than with big slices.

Makes 2 servings

1$^{1}/_{2}$ ripe bananas

1 ripe peach, peeled and diced

1$^{1}/_{4}$ cups yogurt

1 tablespoon maple syrup

$^{1}/_{4}$ cup muesli or granola

Blackberries or raspberries for
   garnish, optional

On the large side of a 4-sided box grater, grate the bananas into a medium bowl. Stir in the peach, yogurt, maple syrup, and muesli. Allow to sit 10 to 15 minutes to soften the cereal. Divide between 2 bowls and top each with a few berries, if desired.

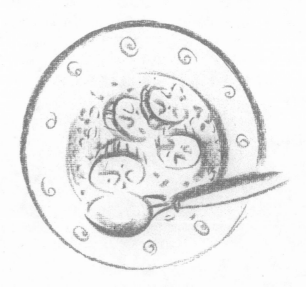

Breakfast Fruit Compote

Prunes, apricots, and bananas seem so sweet and right together. Baking them intensifies their flavors. This is a warm and comforting side dish to serve for a brunch buffet, or spoon up a bowl all for yourself and drizzle it with light cream.

Makes 6 to 8 servings

1 cup dried, pitted prunes

1 cup dried apricots

1/4 cup golden raisins

2 firm-ripe bananas, cut into chunks

Grated zest of 1 orange

2 tablespoons honey

1/2 cup orange juice

2 tablespoons butter

1/4 teaspoon freshly grated nutmeg

The night before, place the prunes and apricots in a small bowl and just cover with boiling water. Cover the bowl and set aside to soak.

Heat the oven to 350°F. Place the prunes, apricots, and the soaking liquid in a medium-size baking dish along with the raisins and bananas. In a small saucepan, heat the zest, honey, orange juice, butter, and nutmeg long enough to dissolve the honey and butter. Pour over the fruit. Bake 30 to 40 minutes, basting occasionally, until the fruit is bubbling hot.

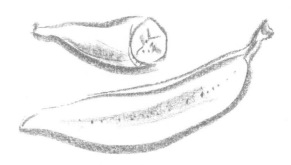

Granola

*Fresh homemade granola tastes
nothing like the overpriced version
that comes in a box. Toasty,
crunchy, and so much better for you
than the fat- and sugar-saturated
variety, this granola can transform
most anyone into a breakfast eater.
You can buy the grains and dried
fruit in bulk at the local health-food
store.*

Makes about 6 cups

$3/4$ cup unsweetened pineapple juice
  (or apple cider)

3 tablespoons canola oil

2 to 3 tablespoons honey

1 teaspoon ground nutmeg

$1/2$ teaspoon ground cinnamon

Pinch of salt

4 cups mixed flakes such as quick-cooking
  oats, wheat, rye, barley, or spelt

$1/4$ cup wheat germ

2 tablespoons oat bran

$1/2$ cup chopped dried (unsalted)
  banana chips

$1/3$ cup chopped almonds or walnuts

$1/4$ cup dried cranberries or cherries

$1/4$ cup chopped dates

$1/4$ cup sweetened, shredded coconut

Heat the oven to 300°F. Lightly spray a large baking sheet with vegetable oil.

Place the pineapple juice, oil, honey, nutmeg, cinnamon, and salt in a small saucepan and heat until the honey is dissolved. Toss together the remaining ingredients in a large bowl. Drizzle the juice mixture over the cereal and stir until the ingredients are evenly moistened.

Spread the granola on the prepared baking sheet. Bake 20 minutes, remove from the oven, and stir and turn the cereal. Bake 20 to 30 minutes longer, or until the granola has turned golden all over (be careful not to overbake). The granola will still seem moist and sticky when you remove it from the oven, but as it dries, it becomes crisp. Store in an airtight container or a freezer bag. It will stay fresh 2 to 3 weeks, or longer if refrigerated or frozen.

Smoothies and Drinks

Here lies the body of our Anna,

Done to death by a banana.

It wasn't the fruit that laid her low,

But the skin of the thing that made her go.

—Epitaph allegedly on a headstone for Anna Hopewell of
Enosburg, Vermont, though none has ever been found and
it is thought to be an urban legend.

Smoothie King

Bananas and peanut butter will forever be linked to Elvis, and you have to wonder if this wouldn't have been his smoothie of choice. Creamy and rich, think of it as a high-powered protein and calcium shake.

Makes 2 drinks

2 frozen ripe bananas, sliced

2 ice cubes

2 cups milk

2 tablespoons peanut butter

1 teaspoon pure vanilla extract

1/4 teaspoon ground cinnamon

Place all ingredients in a blender and purée until smooth. Sprinkle with more cinnamon, if desired.

Strawberry-Banana Smoothie

Probably the most classic smoothie combination. Use this as a basic recipe; you can substitute any berry or fruit for the strawberries.

Makes 2 drinks

1 frozen ripe banana, sliced

1 cup frozen sliced strawberries

1 cup fresh orange juice

1/2 cup yogurt

2 ice cubes

Honey to taste

Place all ingredients in a blender and purée until smooth and thick.

Breakfast in a Glass

Nutritious, low in fat, and very tasty, this is a great drink for breakfast on the run or an afternoon pick-me-up. To make it extra creamy, freeze the fruit before blending.

Makes 2 drinks

4 ripe apricots or 2 peaches, pitted and sliced

2 ripe bananas, sliced

1 cup yogurt

3 tablespoons honey

1/4 cup fresh orange juice

1 tablespoon brewer's yeast, optional

6 ice cubes

Place all ingredients in a blender and purée until smooth. Pour into 2 glasses.

Banana-Mango Batidos

Latin Americans have been sipping smoothies for decades, only they call them batidos (bah-TEE-dohs). They're usually made with milk, ice, and tropical fruit and served at juice stands or at lunch counters. Bananas alone make a delicious drink but try mixing in some of your other favorite fruits.

Makes 2 drinks

1 ripe banana, diced

1 cup ripe mango chunks

1 cup ice-cold milk

3 ice cubes

Place all ingredients in a blender and purée until smooth. Pour into 2 stemmed glasses.

Caramel-Banana Milkshake

An ultrathick shake made with caramel ice cream (you can also use vanilla) that tastes like buttery bananas. Divine!

Makes 2 drinks

2 frozen ripe bananas, sliced

2 large scoops dulce de leche (caramel) ice cream, preferably Häagen-Dazs

1 teaspoon pure vanilla extract

1/4 to 1/2 cup milk

Combine ingredients in a blender, adding just enough milk to make the shake drinkable through a straw.

Frozen Banana Mochaccino

Coffee, banana, chocolate—the world's three most popular flavors combined in one creamy drink. Great for breakfast or dessert.

Makes 2 drinks

2 frozen ripe bananas, sliced

4 ice cubes

1 cup milk

1/2 cup espresso, or very strong coffee, chilled

2 teaspoons sugar, or to taste

2 tablespoons chocolate syrup

Whipped cream and cocoa powder, optional

Place all ingredients except for whipped cream in a blender and purée until smooth. Garnish with whipped cream and cocoa powder, if desired.

Pineapple-Banana Refresher

Have glasses filled with ice cubes and fresh mint ready for this great thirst quencher. It's perfect for a hot day by the pool.

Makes 6 drinks

2 cups fresh orange juice

1 firm-ripe banana, chopped

1/2 cup fresh lemon juice

3 cups unsweetened pineapple juice

Grenadine syrup to taste

Fresh mint sprigs

Place the orange juice and banana in a blender and purée until the banana is liquefied. Pour the banana mixture into a pitcher, adding the lemon juice, pineapple juice, and a few dashes of grenadine to taste. Pour into glasses filled with ice and fresh mint.

Thai Banana Icey

A light, refreshing iced drink with just a hint of the cooling flavor of basil.

Makes 2 drinks

2 ripe bananas

10 ice cubes

2 to 3 tablespoons honey

2 or 3 Thai or Italian basil leaves

Place all ingredients in a blender and purée until smooth. Serve in chilled stemmed glasses and garnish with basil.

Anna Banana

Slightly sweet and luscious.

Makes 2 drinks

3 ounces ($^1/_3$ cup) vodka

4 tablespoons fresh lime juice

1 ripe banana

2 teaspoons honey

6 ice cubes

Lime slices for garnish

Place all ingredients except garnish in a blender and purée until just smooth. Pour into 2 chilled glasses and garnish with lime slices.

Banana-Orange Mimosas

These banana-flavored mimosas are the perfect party drink for a wedding shower or brunch.

Makes 12 drinks

3 cups fresh orange juice, chilled

1 ripe banana

3 tablespoons banana liqueur

1 bottle dry sparkling wine or champagne, chilled

Place the orange juice, banana, and liqueur in a blender and purée until smooth. Fill champagne flutes halfway with juice. Add sparkling wine to fill the glass and serve.

Smoothies and Drinks

Frozen Banaquiris

Banana daquiris are the queen of all banana drinks. I whirred these up in the blender the entire summer I spent working on this book. A friend and I taste-tested so many one night that we dropped a few syllables and renamed them "banaquiris."

Makes 2 drinks

3 ounces ($^1/_3$ cup) light rum

2 teaspoons confectioners' sugar

3 tablespoons fresh lime juice

1 ounce (2 tablespoons) triple sec
   or banana liqueur

1 ripe banana

12 ice cubes

Banana or lime slices for garnish

Place all ingredients in a blender and purée until smooth and thick. Pour into 2 chilled stemmed glasses. Garnish with a banana or lime slice.

Island Sparkler

This is my favorite party drink. The bubbles dance across your tongue, and the rum and liqueur make it smooth and lethal—so delicious it's dangerous.

Makes 2 drinks

Chilled white or rose sparkling wine

1 ounce (2 tablespoons) light rum

4 teaspoons banana liqueur

2 slices finger banana for garnish

Fill 2 champagne flutes nearly to the brim with sparkling wine. Divide rum and banana liqueur between the 2 glasses. Float a banana slice in each drink.

Spice Rum and Banana Punch

A great party punch. This potent and tasty elixir is also quite pretty served from a large glass punch bowl and decorated with floating orange slices and thinly sliced baby bananas.

Makes 6 to 8 drinks

1^1/$_2$ cups fresh orange juice

1^1/$_2$ cups unsweetened pineapple juice

1^1/$_2$ cups mango nectar

^{3}/$_4$ cup dark, spice-flavored rum, or to taste

1 tablespoon banana liqueur

1^1/$_2$ teaspoons angostura bitters

3 tablespoons light brown sugar

1 teaspoon freshly grated nutmeg

1 or 2 finger bananas, thinly sliced lengthwise

1 large navel orange, thinly sliced

Pour the juices, rum, banana liqueur, bitters, brown sugar, and nutmeg into a large punch bowl and stir gently until the sugar is dissolved. (You can make the punch ahead of time and refrigerate until you're ready to serve.) Fill with ice cubes and gently stir in the banana and orange slices. Ladle the punch with a little fruit into the glasses.

Strawberry-Banana Margarita

I'm usually a purist when it comes to margaritas, but the bananas and strawberries make this tangy-sweet drink even better.

Makes 2 drinks

1 cup chopped strawberries, frozen

1 ripe banana, frozen

4^1/$_2$ ounces (^{1}/$_2$ cup plus 1 tequila

1^1/$_2$ ounces (3 tablespoons) triple sec

2 tablespoons fresh lime or lemon juice

6 ice cubes

Strawberry and banana slices for garnish

Place all ingredients in a blender except garnish and blend until smooth but still very thick. Pour into 2 chilled margarita or other stemmed glasses.

Banana-Rum Fizzes

Banana floats for adults. Serve them for dessert.

Makes 2 drinks

1 cup vanilla ice cream

1 ripe banana

1 ounce (2 tablespoons) crème de cacao or banana liqueur

2 ounces (4 tablespoons) dark rum, or to taste

³⁄₄ cup club soda or seltzer, chilled

Banana slices for garnish

Place ice cream and banana in a blender and purée until smooth but still thick. Pour into 2 chilled stemmed glasses. Divide crème de cacao and rum between the 2 glasses. Pour in club soda and garnish with banana slices. Serve with long spoons and straws.

Banshee

A creamy cocktail that makes a sweet nightcap.

Makes 2 drinks

2 ounces (4 tablespoons) crème de cacao

2 ounces (4 tablespoons) banana liqueur

2 ounces (4 tablespoons) half-and-half

Freshly grated nutmeg and banana slices for garnish

Place crème de cacao, banana liqueur, and half-and-half in a cocktail shaker filled with ice. Shake and pour into 2 chilled stemmed glasses. Grate a little nutmeg in each and place a banana slice on the rim.

Banana Colada

Creamy, cool, and potent. The banana adds a sweet touch to this otherwise authentic piña colada. Straws required.

Makes 2 drinks

$1/2$ cup unsweetened pineapple juice

1 ripe banana

2 tablespoons fresh lime juice

3 ounces ($1/3$ cup) cream of coconut

3 ounces ($1/3$ cup) light rum

6 ice cubes

Maraschino cherries, grated coconut, and orange slices for garnish

Place all ingredients except garnishes in a blender and purée until smooth and thick. Pour into chilled, tall stemmed glasses. Place cherry, coconut, and orange slices on top and serve with a straw.

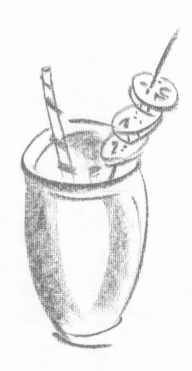

Salads, Soups, and Sandwiches

"Oh the delicious fruits that we have here and in Syria!

Orange gardens miles in extent, citrons, limes, pomegranates;

but the most delicious thing in the world is a banana, which

is richer than a pineapple."

—Benjamin Disraeli, in a letter to his sister from Cairo, dated 1831

Asian Spiced Fruit

Southeast Asian cooks have a great talent for juxtaposing flavors to create unexpected combinations. Here, hot chiles, pepper, gingerroot, and spices lift tropical fruit to new heights. You can experiment by adding other fruits such as kiwi, pear, star fruit, or tart green apple. Serve this as a first course, alongside rotisserie chicken or poached fish fillets, or spoon it over coconut sorbet for dessert.

Makes 6 to 8 servings

1/3 cup fresh orange juice

2 tablespoons honey, or to taste

3 tablespoons fresh lime juice

1 1/2 tablespoons finely minced gingerroot

1 to 2 small red chiles, seeded and finely minced

1/2 teaspoon ground white pepper

1/2 teaspoon ground cinnamon

1/4 teaspoon ground cardamom

Pinch of ground cloves

2 ripe mangoes, peeled, seeded, and diced

2 ripe red bananas (or yellow), diced

1 large, ripe papaya, peeled, seeded, and diced

2 ripe peaches, peeled and diced

1/2 ripe pineapple, peeled, cored, and diced

Fresh mint

In a small bowl, whisk together the orange juice, honey, lime juice, gingerroot, chiles, pepper, cinnamon, cardamom, and cloves. Toss with the fruit in a serving bowl. Cover the bowl with plastic wrap and refrigerate 2 to 3 hours. Garnish with mint leaves before serving.

Avocado, Grapefruit, and Banana Salad with Banana-Poppyseed Dressing

A refreshing citrus and fruit salad on its own, but add a wedge of gorgonzola, feta, or goat cheese, and it becomes a great lunch.

Makes 4 servings

1 large bunch arugula or watercress, rinsed, dried, and tough stems removed

1 ripe Haas avocado, thinly sliced and brushed with lemon juice to prevent darkening

1 red grapefruit, peeled and sectioned

2 firm-ripe finger bananas, sliced lengthwise

1/2 medium red onion, thinly sliced

Dressing:

1 firm-ripe banana, mashed

3/4 cup yogurt, preferably whole-milk

1/4 cup extra virgin olive oil

1 shallot, finely minced

2 tablespoons coarsely chopped cilantro or parsley

1 tablespoon brown sugar

1 tablespoon rice wine vinegar

1 teaspoon red wine vinegar

2 tablespoons fresh orange juice

1 tablespoon poppy seeds

1/2 teaspoon kosher salt

1/4 teaspoon freshly milled pepper

Arrange arugula on four plates. Divide the avocado, grapefruit, banana, and onion slices between the plates and arrange on top of the greens. (You can assemble salads to this point, cover with plastic wrap, and refrigerate until ready to serve.)

Place dressing ingredients in a blender and pulse a few times until thoroughly mixed (or whisk together in a bowl). Drizzle over salad and save any leftover dressing for future use.

Banana Blossom Salad

In South America the male flowers of the banana plant are sliced off the stem with a machete and left on the ground to compost. But in some Asian countries the large, red buds are used in a variety of dishes—in stir-fries, as a garnish for soups, or in salads. Some banana buds are tastier than others (it depends on the variety), but most people think they taste like a cross between an artichoke and endive. (See page 14 for more details on blossoms.) This salad is quite good with meat or fish and rice. Use rubber gloves when handling the raw blossom because it can stain your hands purple.

Makes 4 servings

1 banana blossom

1 cup canned coconut milk, stir well

2 teaspoons grated gingerroot

1 shallot, thinly sliced

1/2 teaspoon sugar

1 tablespoon red wine vinegar

2 tablespoons fresh lemon juice

2 teaspoons *nuoc mam* (fish sauce), or 1 teaspoon soy sauce

Salt

Freshly milled black pepper

Peel the blossom down to the soft, pale pink inner petals. Slice it lengthwise into 4 pieces. Bring a pot of salted water to a boil and add the blossom pieces. Boil until tender, about 15 minutes.

Drain the blossom and allow it to cool. When it's cool enough to handle, squeeze out any excess water. Shred the blossom by hand into a bowl and discard inner, tough core and seeds, if any. Combine the coconut milk, gingerroot, shallot, and sugar in a small saucepan and bring to a simmer. Cook 10 minutes and remove from heat. Stir in the vinegar, lemon juice, fish sauce, and add salt and pepper to taste. Pour over the blossom and toss. Serve hot.

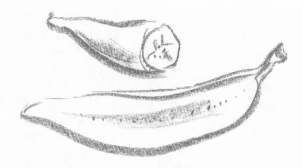

Ensalada de Noche Buena

Mexican Christmas Eve Salad

This makes a beautiful centerpiece as well as a delicious salad for a holiday or other special occasion. Arrange the brilliantly colored fruit and beets in a circular pattern on a large, lettuce-lined platter. Brush the apples and bananas liberally with lime or lemon juice to prevent them from turning brown.

Makes 4 to 6 servings

1 small head Bibb lettuce, leaves separated

1 bunch arugula, rinsed, dried, tough stems removed

1 Granny Smith apple

1 Red Delicious apple

Juice of 2 limes or 1 lemon

2 medium bananas

2 medium navel oranges, peeled and white membrane cut away, sliced thinly into circles

Half a fresh pineapple, peeled, cored, and sliced

2 medium beets, cooked until tender, peeled and sliced

$1/2$ cup chopped unsalted, roasted peanuts

Seeds of half a pomegranate, optional

Dressing:

$1/3$ cup extra virgin olive oil

2 tablespoons lime or lemon juice

1 teaspoon sugar

$1/4$ teaspoon salt

Pinch of ground cumin

Pinch of ground cayenne

Arrange the lettuce and arugula leaves on a large platter. Core and slice the apples and brush with lime juice. Peel and slice the bananas, and brush banana slices with lime juice. Arrange the sliced fruit and beets in concentric circles on the platter, slightly overlapping. Sprinkle the top with the peanuts and pomegranate seeds, if using. (The salad can be assembled to this point and refrigerated about 1 hour before serving. Whisk together the dressing ingredients. Wait until just before serving to drizzle the dressing over the salad. Serve the salad slightly chilled or at room temperature.

Cream of Banana Soup

This is a comforting, thick and creamy soup with a subtle banana sweetness and a bit of heat from the habañero sauce. It is such a simple soup to make, yet is an unusually delicious combination. I love serving it to guests and having them guess what it is.

Makes 4 servings

4 ripe bananas, cut into chunks

2 teaspoons habañero hot sauce (or Scotch bonnet pepper sauce)

2 cups chicken broth

1/2 cup heavy cream

Salt

Freshly milled black pepper

Fresh cilantro leaves

Lime wedges

Place the banana and hot sauce in a food processor or blender and purée until smooth. Transfer to a medium saucepan and whisk in the broth and 1 cup of water. Bring the mixture to a boil; lower the heat and simmer, stirring occasionally, 10 minutes. Skim the foam that rises to the top. Add the cream and return to a boil, stirring. Remove the soup from the heat and add salt and pepper to taste. Ladle into soup bowls and garnish with cilantro and a squeeze of lime juice.

"Australians use the term 'banana oil' in the same sense as Americans say 'snake-oil salesman.' The British colloquialism 'to feel a right 'nana' means to feel foolish.... The term 'top banana' of an organization (rapidly being displaced in popular slang by 'top gun') is supposedly derived from a music-hall routine in which a trio of comedians take turns delivering the punch line while waving a banana. From this came 'second banana,' a deputy or underling. 'Going bananas' is the herbal equivalent of 'going nuts,' perhaps connected with the manhandling meted out to the 'third banana' in music-hall routines."

—Mary Reid, 1992, *Fruits and Nuts in Symbolism and Celebration*

Plantain and Sweet Potato Soup

Although based on a Brazilian recipe, this soup probably originated in Africa. The ham broth adds a wonderful, smoky flavor to the soup, which is hearty enough to serve for dinner. It's perfect for a brisk, fall evening served with a fresh cabbage and carrot salad.

Makes 6 servings

2 large ham hocks

1 large onion

3 whole cloves

1/2 teaspoon ground allspice

1 bay leaf

2 large sweet potatoes, peeled
   and cut into cubes

3 ripe, black-skinned plantains

1 Granny Smith apple, peeled,
   cored, and diced

1 teaspoon dried thyme

3 tablespoons butter

Salt

Freshly milled ground pepper

2 tablespoons fresh minced chives
   or parsley

Cover the ham hocks in a large pot with about 6 cups of water. Stud the onion with the cloves and add it to the pot along with the allspice and bay leaf. Bring the mixture to a boil, then reduce the heat and simmer for 1 hour, occasionally skimming the foam and fat from the top. Remove the ham hocks, reserving them, and strain the broth (if desired, refrigerate the broth and remove the fat that accumulates on top, or use a skimming cup to drain off the broth).

Place the potatoes, plantains, apple, and thyme in a large saucepan and add enough broth to cover. Bring to a boil, then reduce the heat to a simmer; cover and cook until tender, about 30 minutes. Transfer the contents to the bowl of a food processor. (You can also use an immersion blender to purée the soup in the pot, if desired.) Purée, in batches if necessary, until smooth. Return the contents to the pot and add more broth, if needed, to thin the soup. Simmer until just heated through. Add the butter and salt and pepper to taste. Dice some of the lean ham-hock meat, and garnish the soup with the ham and chives.

Sancocho

Chicken, Plantain, and Hominy Soup

Sancocho is from the Spanish verb sancochar, which means "to parboil." It is applied to a number of South American dishes that are similar to a boiled dinner of meats and vegetables. Sancocho can be anything from a simple soup to a large party dish for a special occasion. This particularly savory soup was inspired by a trip to Bolivar, a Pan American restaurant in Manhattan that specializes in South American cuisines. Chef Larry Kolar shared his recipe, simplified for the home cook.

Makes 4 to 6 servings

4 cups chicken broth (low sodium, if using canned)

2 chicken breast halves (bones in)

3 tablespoons olive oil

1 cup diced Spanish onion

2 garlic cloves, minced

1 serrano chile, seeded and finely sliced

$1/2$ cup sliced red bell pepper

$1/2$ large green plantain (or 1 green banana), diced

1 medium sweet potato, peeled, diced, and parboiled

One 15.5-ounce can white hominy, rinsed and drained

2 cups unsweetened canned coconut milk, stir well

2 plum tomatoes, seeded and chopped

Salt

Freshly milled black pepper

Garnish: diced avocado tossed in lime juice, chopped serrano chiles, lime wedges, and fresh cilantro

Place the broth and 2 cups of water in a 2-quart pot. Bring to a boil and add the chicken. Reduce the heat and simmer 15 to 20 minutes, or until the chicken is just cooked through. Remove the chicken to a plate to cool. Reserve the broth. When cool, remove the skin from the chicken and debone. Slice the chicken into 1-inch pieces.

Heat the oil in a large, deep saucepan over medium heat. Add the onion, garlic, chile, and bell pepper and cook, stirring, 5 to 8 minutes, or until just tender. Add the broth and bring to a boil. Add the plantain, sweet potato, and hominy to the broth. Reduce the heat and simmer 20 minutes, or until the plantain and sweet potato are tender. Add the sliced chicken, coconut milk, tomatoes, and salt and pepper to taste. Remove from heat. Ladle into deep soup bowls. Serve with avocado, more chile (if desired), a squeeze of lime, and cilantro leaves.

Grilled PB&B

My friend Margo True, then a fledgling food writer in Houston, Texas, remembers with fondness a restaurant she once reviewed called The King, which featured all the food that Elvis loved. The most popular item on the menu, not surprisingly, was the grilled peanut butter and banana sandwich. It's also the best-selling item at New York's Peanut Butter & Co., a cozy cafe devoted to all things peanutty. It's great for breakfast or lunch with an ice-cold glass of milk—or a milk shake.

Makes 1 sandwich

2 slices country-style white bread

2 to 3 tablespoons peanut butter

$1/2$ ripe banana, thinly sliced

Softened butter

Honey, jam or jelly, optional

Heat a heavy-bottomed skillet over medium heat. Spread the bread with the peanut butter and top with banana slices and slice of bread. Spread both sides well with butter. Place the sandwich in the hot skillet. Grill until the bread is golden brown on the bottom. Flip the sandwich and press down on the top with a spatula to flatten it. When the bottom is golden brown, remove the sandwich to a cutting board, cut in half, and top with honey or jam, if desired.

Other banana-sandwich ideas:

Grilled mozzarella, smoked turkey, and banana with honey mustard on pumpernickel bread.

Peanut butter, bacon, and banana on cinnamon-raisin bread.

Grilled ham, banana, and pepper Jack cheese on rye bread.

Cream cheese, bananas, and chopped pecans on date bread.

Toasted French bread, Nutella, and thin banana slices.

Appetizers and Nibbles

"Pomegranates come from red hot pearls.

Cherries are the hearts of baby girls.

Persimmons come up on the bosom of dawn.

Plums fill the sky when the day is gone.

Pineapples grow on the heads of kings.

Bananas are nothing but naughty things."

From "Fruits of Experience," by James Broughton

Banana and Bean Dip

This recipe comes from Ecuador and is usually made with sausage, but I prefer the vegetarian version. Bananas lighten the heavy beans and make an irresistible party dip.

Makes about 4 cups

2 tablespoons canola oil

1 medium red onion, chopped

2 garlic cloves, minced

2 poblano or sweet Italian peppers, seeded and chopped

1/2 cup canned tomato sauce

4 firm-ripe bananas

2 cups cooked kidney beans, rinsed, drained, and slightly mashed

Shredded Monterey Jack cheese, optional

Tortilla chips

Heat the oil in a large skillet over medium heat. Cook the onion, garlic, and peppers until soft. Stir in the tomato sauce and cook 3 minutes, stirring. Add the bananas and cook until just heated through, about 2 to 3 minutes. Remove from the heat and add the beans. Mash the ingredients together with a potato masher, adding a little warm water to make it a "dip" consistency. Return to low heat and cook until the dip is just heated through. Sprinkle the top with cheese, if desired. Serve warm with tortilla chips.

Tostones with Caribbean Dipping Sauce

Fried Green Plantains

Caribbean Dipping Sauce
  (recipe follows)
4 green plantains

Vegetable oil for frying
Kosher salt

With a sharp knife, trim the ends from the plantains and cut them in half crosswise. Cut a shallow slit through the skin inside the curve of each piece. Pry the skin away from the plantain with your fingers. (See plantain peeling tips, page 13.) Cut into large, diagonal slices about 1-inch thick (reserve the peels for flattening the tostones later).

In an electric skillet, deep fryer, or a large pot with a thermometer attached, heat about $1\frac{1}{2}$ inches of oil to 375°F. Fry the plantain pieces in batches until they are golden on both sides, about 2 minutes per side. Transfer with a slotted spoon to paper towels to drain and cool.

Once all the pieces are fried, place pieces, one at a time, between 2 plantain peels or several thicknesses of paper towels. Press down on them with the ball of your hand to flatten to a $\frac{1}{4}$-inch thickness. Repeat until all slices have been pressed and flattened. (You can keep the slices at room temperature for 2 hours until you're ready to refry and serve them, place them in the refrigerator for several days, or even freeze the slices for several weeks.)

Return the plantain pieces to the hot oil and fry, turning occasionally, for 2 to 3 more minutes, or until golden brown. Transfer to fresh paper towels to drain. Sprinkle lightly with salt. Serve immediately with the dipping sauce, if desired, or hold the slices in a 200°F oven for 30 minutes.

Caribbean Dipping Sauce

Please wear rubber gloves when mincing a Scotch bonnet pepper—they're the most lethally hot of all the chile peppers.

1 shallot, finely minced

2 garlic cloves, finely minced

1/4 cup finely diced red bell pepper

1 Scotch bonnet chile, seeded and finely minced (or 1 teaspoon Scotch bonnet or habañero hot pepper sauce)

1 teaspoon salt

1 tablespoon brown sugar

1/2 cup white vinegar

2 tablespoons canola oil

2 tablespoons chopped fresh coriander

Place all ingredients in a bowl and whisk together until sugar is dissolved. Serve with hot tostones.

Mofongo

Plantain and Pork Balls

In this Puerto Rican dish, sweet plantains and fried pork rinds are combined to make savory, meatball-shaped snacks that are eaten alone or with a spicy tomato sauce. They can be flattened as cakes and served with chicken or pork for a main dish. Mofongo can also be stuffed with cooked meat or seafood. I think they're great plain, enjoyed with an icy cold beer. Chicharrones are large, puffed up, fried pork rinds that are superior to the puny, tough ones I grew up with in the South. You can generally find them packaged in large bags in Latin American neighborhoods. If not, use the domestic ones but discard any hard ones. Fitting the pork rinds into the food processor is tricky, so this is what I do: Place the bag of pork rinds in another, larger plastic bag (a supermarket bag works well), and lay it on your kitchen floor. Gently tap the bag with your feet until the pork rinds are small, crumbled bits. Add the crushed rinds in batches with the plantains.

Makes 4 to 6 servings

Vegetable oil for frying
5 ripe, soft yellow-skinned
    plantains
1 (5- or 6-ounce bag) fried pork
    rinds *(chicharrones)*
4 large garlic cloves, minced
Salt

Heat about 1 inch of oil in a large skillet over medium-high heat. Peel and slice the plantains into 1/3-inch-thick slices. Fry the plantains on both sides until soft and tender, about 3 minutes per side. Transfer to a tray lined with paper towels to drain.

Crush the pork rinds in a plastic bag. Place about a third of them in a bowl of a food processor along with a third of the plantains and some of the garlic. Process until the mixture is well blended and forms a sticky dough. Season with salt. Repeat with the remaining ingredients, mixing all the dough together in a large bowl so that the ingredients are evenly distributed.

Preheat the oven to 350°F. Using your hands, roll and pat the dough to form balls about 2 inches in diameter (about the size of small limes). Place on a large baking sheet sprayed with cooking oil. Bake 5 to 10 minutes, until the *mofongo* are very hot. Serve them alone or with a hearty stew. Makes about 12 *mofongo* balls.

Bacon and Banana Kabobs

Slightly sweet and tangy from the honey mustard, these bacon and banana nibbles are so good you may want to double the recipe just to have leftovers to snack on later. These kabobs can also be grilled.

Makes 4 to 6 servings

1^1/$_2$ tablespoons Dijon mustard

1 tablespoon honey

1^1/$_2$ tablespoons lemon juice

Salt

Freshly milled black pepper

3 firm-ripe bananas

12 slices bacon

Soak twelve 10-inch wooden skewers in warm water for 30 minutes. In a small bowl, combine the mustard, honey, and lemon juice with salt and pepper to taste. Slice the bananas crosswise into 8 pieces, add to the bowl with the mustard mixture, and toss to coat. Allow to marinate 30 minutes.

Meanwhile, cook the bacon in a large skillet until browned but still limp enough to handle. Transfer to paper towels to cool. Slice each piece in half. Wrap each banana piece with bacon and thread onto skewers, 2 pieces per skewer. Preheat the oven broiler (or grill, if desired). Place kabobs on a baking sheet lightly sprayed with cooking oil. Broil about 4 inches away from the heat source, 5 to 8 minutes, turning occasionally, until the bacon is crisp and browned.

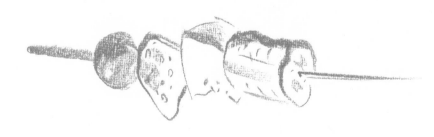

Chile-Dusted Green Banana Chips

I was sitting at a bar waiting for a friend one evening on the Caribbean island of St. Lucia when the bartender offered me a bowl of hot chips. They were so amazing I ate them all, leaving none for my friend. I had never eaten a banana cooked this way before; it was a revelation. They're amazingly simple to make and sure to be a hit at any party. A mandoline, or one of those handy vegetable-slicing gadgets (such as a V-Slicer), makes quick work of slicing both variations of this recipe, though a sharp knife and a careful eye will also do. Figure on 1 banana per person. Also, banana or plantain "tongues," sliced lengthwise into long strips, are popular snacks throughout South America. Similar to the chips, these wonderful appetizers can be passed around standing up in parchment-lined pilsner glasses.

Makes 4 to 6 servings

Vegetable oil for frying

4 to 6 green bananas

1 teaspoon chile powder

1 teaspoon salt

Heat about 3 inches of oil in an electric skillet, deep fryer, or a large pot with a thermometer attached to 350°F. Peel the bananas (green-banana peeling tips, page 13). Use a mandoline, vegetable slicer, or sharp knife to slice the bananas into thin circles, about ⅛-inch thick. Soak them in ice water 15 minutes, or up to 2 hours ahead. Dry thoroughly with paper towels before frying.

Line a large baking sheet with several layers of paper towels. Working in batches, fry a few banana slices at a time, turning if necessary, until they're crisp and golden brown, about 1 to 1½ minutes. Transfer to the paper-lined baking sheet to drain. Stir together the chile powder and salt; sprinkle chips with the salt mixture and serve immediately.

Variation

Fried banana or plantain tongues: Slice green bananas or plantains lengthwise with a mandoline, vegetable slicer, or a very sharp vegetable peeler. Soak in ice water and dry well. Fry a few at a time as directed above and sprinkle with salt. Serve hot or room temperature.

Spicy Plantain French Fries

These crunchy coated plantains will remind you a bit of sweet potato fries, and they're just as addictive. Though the fries are delicious without the added spices and just a bit of salt, the spices give them a little barbecue flavor. They make great appetizers (try them with ketchup or homemade mayonnaise), or you can serve them on the side with your favorite cut of steak. Minus the cayenne, they're also extremely toddler friendly. This recipe is based on one created by cookbook author Nicole Routhier.

Serves 4 to 6

Vegetable oil for frying

2 large eggs

2 tablespoons milk

1³/4 cups dried bread crumbs

1 teaspoon chile powder

¹/4 teaspoon cayenne pepper

4 ripe (mottled yellow and slightly
   soft) plantains

Kosher salt

Heat at least 3 inches of oil in an electric skillet, deep fryer, or a large pot with a thermometer attached to 350°F.

Beat the eggs and milk in a shallow bowl. In another shallow bowl, stir together the bread crumbs, chile powder, and cayenne.

Slice the ends of the plantains and remove the peels. Cut the plantains in half, then half lengthwise. Slice each quarter into 3 or 4 long sticks, about ¹/2-inch thick. Dip each plantain stick first in the egg mixture, then coat evenly in the bread crumbs. Arrange coated sticks on a large baking sheet. (Fries can be dipped and coated a few hours ahead of serving time, kept covered with plastic wrap, and refrigerated until ready to cook.)

Line another large baking sheet with several layers of paper towels. Working in batches, fry a few plantain sticks at a time, turning if necessary, until the fries are crisp and golden brown, about 1¹/2 to 2 minutes. Transfer to the paper-lined baking sheet to drain. Sprinkle with salt and serve immediately.

Join the Club and Go Bananas

*I*n 1972, photographer Ken Bannister founded The International Banana Club, a philan-thropic organization dedicated to "making the world a nicer place," and if that makes Bannister seem a little...bananas, well then so be it. At least he's not nuts!

Club members are "known for their desire to maintain a sense of humor and have fun in an otherwise hectic world, and to bring a smile to those around them." The club offers titles to everyone who joins. You can choose your own title: for instance, C.H.D., F.D., and R.R.B. stand for City Hand Director, Finger Director, and Real Ripe Banana, respectively. Or make up one of your own. Members can earn B.M.'s (banana merits) for sending banana-related items to the club's memorabilia-stuffed museum in Altadena, California. However, nothing lewd or crude is accepted. Good deeds can earn members a Master of Bananistry or even a full doctorate.

You can start your own Banana Club franchise. (For more information, see Sources, page 182.)

Green Plantain Turnovers

These can be stuffed with meat filling, refried beans, or filled with
cream cheese, dusted with confectioners' sugar, and served as a sweet.
You can make them up several days
in advance of a party and freeze
them. Let them thaw at room temperature for about 20 minutes before frying.

Makes 4 to 6 servings

1 recipe Picadillo Filling, page 76

3 green to semiripe plantains

2 tablespoons butter

1 large egg, beaten

¼ cup all-purpose flour

Salt

Freshly milled black pepper

Vegetable oil for frying

Bring a large pot of salted water to a boil. Cut off the ends of the
plantains and cut into 4 pieces. Boil 15 minutes, or until tender.
Remove from the heat and cool. Slice off the peels. Place the plantains, butter, egg, flour, and salt and pepper to taste in the bowl of a
food processor and pulse until it forms a smooth dough. If necessary,
add a little milk or flour to get it to the proper consistency. Turn the
dough out onto a piece of plastic wrap and shape into a large disk.
Wrap tightly and refrigerate at least 30 minutes.

Lightly flour your hands. On a lightly floured surface, press about
⅓ cup of dough into a small circle, about 3 inches in diameter. Place
a small amount of the meat filling in the center. Fold the turnover in
half and press or crimp the edges together to form a half-moon shape.
Repeat with the remaining dough and filling (you may have some filling left over). Place the turnovers on a tray and refrigerate them at
least 30 minutes (or turnovers can be prepared to this point and
frozen until ready to use).

Heat at least 3 inches of oil in an electric skillet, deep fryer, or a
large pot with a thermometer attached to 350°F.

Line a large baking sheet with several layers of paper towels and
heat the oven to 200°F. Working in batches, fry a few turnovers at a
time, turning if necessary, until they are golden brown, 2 to 4 minutes. Transfer to the paper-lined baking sheet to drain and place in
the oven to keep warm while you fry the remaining turnovers.

Plantain Galettes

These wonderful little appetizers will remind you of sweet potato pancakes. Try them topped with a dollop of sour cream and a bit of caviar or with sautéed baby spinach with bits of bacon.

Makes 8 to 10 servings

4 ripe, black-skinned plantains

1 tablespoon minced fresh thyme, plus more for garnish

2 garlic cloves, minced

1 large egg

1/3 cup fresh orange juice

1 teaspoon salt

1/4 teaspoon freshly milled black pepper

Pinch of cayenne

1/2 cup plus 2 tablespoons all-purpose flour

1/3 to 1/2 cup milk

4 tablespoons canola oil

Salt

Sour cream for garnish

Preheat the oven to 350°F. Line a baking dish with foil and place the plantains, skins on, in the dish. Prick the skins with a sharp knife a few times to allow steam to escape. Bake about 35 minutes, or until plantains are soft and puffed looking (alternately, prick the skins and place in a microwave oven on high power for 5 minutes, turning occasionally to cook evenly). Remove the skins and mash plantains with a fork in a bowl until smooth (you can also purée the pulp in the bowl of a food processor). You should have around 2 cups of purée. Add the thyme, garlic, egg, orange juice, salt, pepper, and cayenne and mix together well. Stir in the flour and enough milk to make the batter smooth but not a sticky paste. (The dough is similar to drop-biscuit batter.)

Heat 1 or 2 tablespoons of the oil in a large skillet over medium-high heat. Using a tablespoon to measure, drop heaping spoonfuls of the batter to form each galette. Cook a few galettes at a time, being careful not to crowd the pan. Cook about 2 minutes on each side, or until golden brown. Keep galettes warm while you cook the rest of the batter, adding more oil if necessary. Before serving, sprinkle with salt and top with a dab of sour cream and some thyme. Makes about 20 galettes.

Bananas for Dinner

"It is a banana, madam," said the rogue....

"Such a thing never grew in Paradise," I said.

"Indeed it did, madam," says he, all puffed up like a poison adder.

"This fruit is from the island of Bermuda, which is closer to

Paradise than you will ever be....

THIS IS NOT SOME UNFORTUNATE RAKE. IT IS THE FRUIT OF A TREE.

IT IS TO BE PEELED AND EATEN."

—Jeanette Winterson, *Sexing the Cherry*

Banana-Stuffed Chicken with Curry Sauce

This Caribbean-inspired dish reminds me of chicken Kiev, but instead of butter inside the crisp, boneless chicken roll, there are soft, sweet bananas. Although there are a few steps to the dish, the chicken rolls and the sauce can be assembled earlier in the day. Just cook the chicken and reheat the sauce before serving. Serve with steamed potatoes or rice as you'll want to mop up all the fruity curry sauce.

Makes 4 servings

4 boneless, skinless, chicken breast
  halves
Salt
Freshly milled black pepper
2 firm-ripe bananas
2 tablespoons butter
2 garlic cloves, minced
1 shallot, minced
1 Granny Smith apple, peeled, cored,
  and finely diced
1 ripe mango, peeled and finely diced
3 teaspoons Madras curry powder

$1/4$ to $1/2$ teaspoon cayenne pepper
Pinch of cinnamon
3 tablespoons all-purpose flour, plus
  more for dredging
$2^{1}/_{2}$ cups low-sodium chicken broth
1 large egg beaten with 2 tablespoons
  water
$1/2$ cup dried bread crumbs
3 tablespoons canola oil
$1/3$ cup unsweetened, canned coconut
  milk, stir well
2 tablespoons chopped cilantro

Unfold each chicken breast half to form a butterfly shape (slicing a little with a knife to fan it out, if necessary). Place each piece of chicken between 2 sheets of plastic wrap, and using the bottom of a heavy skillet or meat mallet, pound to about a $1/3$-inch thickness. Sprinkle with salt and pepper. Cut the bananas in half and slice again in half lengthwise. Arrange 2 slices in the center of each chicken breast, fold in the ends, and roll up the chicken to enclose the banana completely. Wrap each chicken roll in plastic wrap and refrigerate at least 1 hour.

Meanwhile, heat the butter over medium heat in a large, deep skillet. Add the garlic and shallot, and sauté until soft. Add the apple, mango, curry powder, cayenne, cinnamon, and flour. Cook, stirring, 1 to 2 minutes. Stir in the broth and bring to a boil. Lower the heat and simmer 20 minutes, or until the apples are completely cooked and the sauce has thickened. Set aside to cool while you cook the chicken.

Preheat the oven to 425°F. Unwrap the chicken breasts and lightly dredge first in flour, then the beaten egg, and then the bread crumbs, coating all sides and ends. Heat the oil in a large, ovenproof skillet or Dutch oven over medium-high heat. Brown the chicken on all sides. Place the skillet in the oven to finish cooking, 15 to 20 minutes, or until the chicken is just cooked through.

To finish the sauce, purée the cooled mixture in a food processor (or with an immersion blender) until smooth. Return to the skillet, add the coconut milk, and bring to a simmer; cook 1 minute, stirring, and season to taste with salt and pepper. Transfer the chicken to plates, spoon some of the sauce over the chicken, and sprinkle with the cilantro.

Brazilian Braised Chicken with Bananas

Makes 4 to 6 servings

3¹/2 to 4 pounds chicken thighs and legs

$3\frac{1}{2}$ to 4 pounds chicken thighs
and legs

$\frac{1}{4}$ cup fresh lemon juice

Salt

Freshly milled black pepper

3 tablespoons vegetable oil

1 medium onion, chopped

6 ripe plum tomatoes, seeded
and chopped

Pinch of sugar

1 cup dry white wine

$\frac{1}{2}$ cup low-sodium chicken broth

3 tablespoons butter

6 firm-ripe bananas, halved
lengthwise

$\frac{1}{2}$ cup grated Parmesan cheese

Rinse the chicken and pat it dry with paper towels. Rub it all over with the lemon juice and sprinkle well with salt and pepper. In a deep, heavy-bottomed skillet or Dutch oven with a lid, heat the oil over medium heat. Brown the chicken on all sides until golden brown. Remove from the skillet and keep warm. Add the onion, tomatoes, and sugar and cook, stirring, until soft. Return the chicken pieces to the skillet, add the wine and broth, and bring to a simmer. Lower the heat and cover. Simmer until the chicken is tender, about 45 minutes. Set aside and keep warm.

In another large skillet, heat the butter and sauté the bananas on both sides until golden brown. Arrange the bananas on top of the chicken in the skillet and sprinkle them with the Parmesan. Turn the heat on low, cover, and cook just until the cheese melts. Use a large spatula to transfer the chicken with bananas on top to plates. Serve immediately.

Curried Beef and Plantain Stew

An African-inspired stew that will please the meat, potato, and curry lover in you. Serve this with lots of buttered egg noodles and a fresh green salad.

Makes 4 to 6 servings

1/4 cup vegetable oil

1 large Spanish onion, thinly sliced

1 1/2 pounds lean stewing beef, such as beef chuck, cut into 1-inch pieces

3 tablespoons all-purpose flour, seasoned with salt and freshly milled black pepper

2 teaspoons hot Madras curry powder

1/4 to 1/2 teaspoon cayenne pepper, depending on taste

1 tablespoon tomato paste

2 medium tomatoes, seeded and chopped

2 ripe, yellow-skinned plantains, or 4 green bananas, peeled and cut into 1/2-inch-thick slices

1 cup canned coconut milk, stir well

Salt

Freshly milled black pepper

1/4 cup chopped fresh cilantro for garnish

Heat the oil in a heavy-bottomed, nonreactive skillet (or Dutch oven) over medium heat. Add the onion and cook, stirring, until soft. Toss the beef in the seasoned flour and add to the onions along with the curry powder and cayenne. Cook the meat, stirring, until browned on all sides. Add 2 cups of cold water, the tomato paste, tomatoes, and plantains. (If using green bananas, wait to add them after the meat is tender.) Bring to a boil. Reduce the heat to low, cover, and simmer 1 to 1 1/2 hours, stirring occasionally, until the meat is fork-tender. If using green bananas, add them at this point and simmer, uncovered, for 20 minutes, or until bananas are just soft but still maintain their shape.

Add the coconut milk and bring to a boil, stirring. Remove from the heat and add salt and pepper to taste. Sprinkle with the cilantro and serve.

Grilled Steak and Banana Kabobs with Pico de Gallo

I think most people like to make kabobs with meat and vegetables because it's attractive. The problem is that not everything cooks at the same rate so you're often left with crunchy onions and overdone meat. My solution: Cook them separately to make sure everything gets done at the same time. Grilled bananas are a sweet foil to this spicy mixed grill. Although quite good on its own, the Pico de Gallo (tomato salsa) really adds the finishing touch to this sensational summer barbecue dinner.

Makes 6 servings

Jerk Spice Rub, page 86
3 tablespoons fresh lime juice
1/2 cup extra virgin olive oil
3 pounds sirloin steak, trimmed
 and cut into 2-inch cubes
4 medium red onions, quartered

2 red bell peppers, seeded and cut
 into 2-inch pieces
5 firm-ripe bananas, peels on, cut
 into 1 1/2-inch-long pieces
Pico de Gallo (recipe follows)

Mix together 3 tablespoons of the spice rub, the lime juice, and olive oil. Toss the sirloin cubes with half the spice marinade and refrigerate at least 30 minutes. Arrange on skewers, leaving a little room between the meat cubes to allow them to cook all around.

Preheat a gas grill to medium-high heat, or prepare a charcoal fire. Place the vegetables and bananas separately on skewers so that the vegetables just touch each other but aren't crammed together. Brush lightly with the remaining marinade. Prick the banana skins lightly with the end of a sharp knife to allow steam to escape. Begin cooking the vegetable and banana skewers first, on a cooler part of the fire, turning as necessary until they are browned and tender all over.

Cook the steak on the hottest part of the grill, about 1 or 2 minutes per side, until all sides are browned. (Test the meat by slicing into a piece to see that it is cooked to desired doneness.)

Remove the meat, vegetables, and bananas from the skewers and arrange on a platter. Serve with Pico de Gallo.

Pico de Gallo

This is a version of the classic salsa served with many Mexican dishes as well as tortilla chips. Try it with a hot batch of tostones.

Makes about 2¹/₂ cups

3 medium tomatoes, seeded and
  finely chopped

¹/₂ cup chopped red onion

1 garlic clove, minced

2 tablespoons fresh lime juice

1 tablespoon extra virgin olive oil

1 to 2 jalapeño peppers, seeded
  and minced

¹/₄ cup chopped fresh cilantro

Salt

Freshly milled black pepper

Mix together all the ingredients in a bowl and add salt and pepper to taste. If desired, add more garlic, onion, or jalapeños to taste.

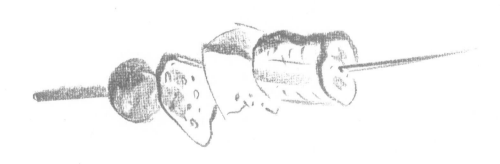

Plátanos Rellenos de Picadillo

Plantains with Picadillo Filling

Serve these stuffed plantains with a dollop of sour cream, Yellow Rice (page 99), and a fresh green salad. They also make delicious appetizers. Making these is kind of a production—it's fun to do with a friend— but they're worth the effort.

Makes 6 to 7 main-course servings, or about 9 appetizer servings

2 tablespoons canola oil, plus
   3 to 4 cups oil for frying

1 medium onion, chopped

2 garlic cloves, minced

2 pounds plum tomatoes, seeded
   and coarsely chopped

1/4 teaspoon ground cinnamon

1/4 teaspoon cayenne pepper

1/2 teaspoon dried oregano

1/4 teaspoon dried thyme

1 bay leaf

1/2 pound ground round, ground
   sirloin, or ground pork

2 tablespoons golden raisins, soaked
   in warm water until softened

10 pimento-stuffed green olives,
   coarsely chopped

7 ripe, soft or black-skinned
   plantains

Coating:

3 large eggs

1 cup all-purpose flour

Salt

Freshly milled black pepper

Heat 2 tablespoons of oil in a large, preferably nonstick skillet over medium heat. Sauté the onion and garlic until the onions are soft, about 4 minutes. Add the tomatoes, cinnamon, cayenne, oregano, thyme, and bay leaf and bring to a simmer. Cook, stirring occasionally, about 10 minutes. Add the meat, breaking up any clumps as it cooks. Stir in the drained raisins and the olives, and cook until the meat is no longer pink. Remove the bay leaf. Remove the pan from the heat and allow the mixture to cool.

Cut the ends off the plantains. Leaving the skin on, slice the plantains crosswise into 1 1/2-inch-long pieces. Using the end of a metal vegetable peeler, hollow out the plantain pieces to form "cups" that will hold the filling. Leave a 1/4-inch-thick "wall" of plantain inside the skin so the cups will be sturdy enough to hold the meat mixture. Spoon a small amount of mixture into each plantain piece, gently but firmly packing the filling into the opening. With a sharp paring knife, make a shallow vertical slit in the skin of each piece; carefully peel off the skin. Place filled, peeled pieces upright in a baking dish so that the meat does not fall out.

Heat the oil in a large electric skillet or deep fat fryer to 350°F. Place several layers of paper towels on a large baking sheet.

To make the coating, beat the eggs well in a medium bowl. Place the flour on a plate and season with salt and pepper. Working in batches, dip the filled plantains in the egg and allow the excess to drip off. Coat each piece with seasoned flour, shaking off excess. Gently lower each piece into the fat with a slotted spoon. Fry several pieces at a time, turning them carefully until they are browned on all sides, about 4 to 5 minutes. Remove with a slotted spoon and drain on paper towels.

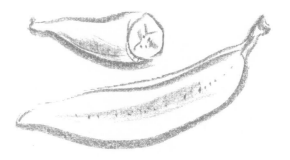

Who is Chiquita Banana?

Chiquita Banana was given life in 1944 by artist Dik Browne. In her early years, Miss Chiquita appeared as an animated banana who told consumers about the nutritional wonder food and how to ripen it. Models and actresses also portrayed the "First Lady of Fruit," as she was called. Puerto Rican–born Elsa Miranda was the most famous Miss Chiquita and made many personal appearances between 1945 and 1946. The likeness of Chiquita Banana has appeared on bananas and other Chiquita products since 1963. In 1987, artist Oscar Grillo—also the creator of the Pink Panther—transformed the banana cartoon into a woman, which reflected the image the public had that Miss Chiquita was a real person.

In 1994, Miss Chiquita celebrated her fiftieth birthday as one of America's most recognized symbols. The woman most recently hired to portray her is Elizabeth Testa of New York, who was chosen in a nationwide search. To celebrate the 100th birthday of the company in 1999, Miss Chiquita received her latest makeover and got a fresh new look for the millennium.

Pork Tenderloin with Glazed Baby Bananas

The bananas taste heavenly baked with pork and coated with sweet-tart, tamarind glaze. You can find tamarind, both fresh and frozen, in Asian markets as well as in super-markets with a large Latin food sec-tion. Tenderloins sometimes come in two long pieces. If so, you'll need to tie the pieces together, side by side, with cotton twine to form a 2-pound roast.

Makes 4 servings

2 pork tenderloins, 1 pound each

3 teaspoons Chinese five-spice powder

Salt

Freshly milled black pepper

$1/4$ cup orange marmalade

$1/4$ cup fresh orange juice

1 tablespoon fresh lime juice

1 tablespoon tamarind pulp, seeds removed (or 1 tablespoon molasses mixed with $1/2$ teaspoon Worcester-shire sauce)

1 tablespoon olive oil

8 to 12 ripe baby bananas

Pat the tenderloins dry with paper towels, then rub them with the spice powder and season with salt and pepper. Set aside 15 minutes. Preheat the oven to 425°F.

Whisk together the marmalade, orange juice, lime juice, and tamarind in a small bowl and set aside. Heat the oil in a large, heavy, ovenproof skillet over medium heat. Brown the tenderloins on all sides and then remove the pan from the heat. Arrange the bananas between and around the tenderloins. Pour the marmalade mixture over the pork and bananas, turning to coat them well. Place the skillet in the oven and roast—basting the meat and bananas once or twice—18 to 20 minutes, or until the temperature of the tenderloins reaches 150°F on a meat thermometer.

Transfer the meat and bananas to a platter and cover loosely with foil (the meat should rest 5 to 10 minutes before carving). Return the skillet to medium heat and add a few tablespoons of water. Heat, stir-ring, until the sauce comes to a simmer. Cook about 3 minutes, or until the sauce has slightly thickened. Add any juices that have accu-mulated on the platter. Season with salt and pepper to taste. Slice the meat and arrange on plates with the bananas. Pour a little of the sauce over each portion. Serve immediately.

Puerto Rican Piñon

Savory Plantain and Beef Casserole

I served this casserole at a dinner party, and because of its many wonderful layers it earned the nickname of "Puerto Rican lasagne." Instead of pasta, the starch is sautéed plantains layered with spicy beef, green beans, and eggs. I love making a big batch for only a few people so that I'll have leftovers to enjoy or freeze for later. Plantains are called for in the authentic version, but you can substitute firm-ripe bananas, which are equally tasty and require no cooking beforehand.

Makes 8 servings

2 tablespoons olive oil

1 medium onion, chopped

1 red bell pepper, diced

3 garlic cloves, minced

1 pound ground sirloin

1 (8-ounce) can tomato sauce

2 tablespoons dark raisins, chopped

2 tablespoons drained Spanish capers

4 large, pimento-stuffed olives, chopped

1 tablespoon red wine vinegar

1 tablespoon sherry or sweet vermouth

2 teaspoons dried oregano

1 teaspoon salt

1/2 teaspoon freshly milled pepper

6 ripe, black-skinned plantains (or 8 to 9 firm-ripe bananas, halved)

Vegetable oil for frying

10 large eggs, beaten with salt and pepper to taste

1 pound green beans, trimmed, cut into 1-inch pieces and steamed until crisp-tender

2 hard-boiled eggs, sliced

1/2 cup grated Parmesan cheese

Heat the oil in a large, 12-inch skillet over medium heat. Add the onion, bell pepper, and garlic and cook, stirring, until the onions are soft. Add the sirloin and cook, breaking up the beef, until it is browned. Add the tomato sauce, raisins, capers, olives, vinegar, sherry, oregano, salt, and pepper. Simmer, stirring occasionally, 20 minutes. Adjust the seasoning and cover to keep warm.

(If using bananas, proceed to the next step). In another large skillet, heat 1 inch of oil over medium heat. Peel the plantains and slice into long, diagonal slices, about 1/3-inch thick. Fry the plantains in the hot oil, turning once, until golden on both sides and soft and tender. Carefully remove with a large, slotted spatula to a baking sheet lined with several layers of paper towels.

Heat the oven to 350°F. Generously butter a 9 x 13 x 2-inch baking dish. Pour half the beaten eggs into the bottom of the baking dish.

Top with half the fried plantain slices (or bananas, if using). Spoon the meat mixture over the plantains and top with the green beans and egg slices. Arrange the remaining plantain slices on top and pour the remaining egg batter to evenly cover the casserole. Bake, uncovered, 35 to 45 minutes, or until the eggs are set. Before removing from the oven, scatter with the Parmesan and broil until the top is golden brown. Cool 5 minutes before slicing into large, lasagne-size squares.

Bananas for Dinner

Ecuadorean Lamb Stew

Many Ecuadorean soups and stews call for mashed bananas, which are added at the last minute to thicken the sauce. Bananas add a touch of sweetness to this vibrantly flavored stew and help balance the acidity of the peppers and lime. To ensure you have the proper degree of heat, buy several jalapeños and use only the hottest ones (test them by touching a little sliver to your tongue). Serve this with rice seasoned with cilantro, lime juice, and a little olive oil.

Makes 6 servings

2 pounds lean, boneless lamb, cut into 1¹/₂-inch pieces
Salt
Freshly milled black pepper
4 garlic cloves, minced
4 tablespoons vegetable oil
1¹/₄ teaspoons ground cumin
3 red bell peppers, seeded and sliced into 1-inch strips
1 large onion, thinly sliced
2 jalapeño chiles, seeded and finely chopped
1 teaspoon dried oregano
1 cup dry white wine
1 cup low-sodium chicken broth
1 lime, quartered
2 large firm-ripe bananas, mashed
¹/₄ cup coarsely chopped cilantro

Season the lamb well with salt and pepper. Scatter the garlic over the meat and toss with 1 tablespoon of the oil and the cumin. Marinate in the refrigerator for at least 30 minutes.

In a large, heavy saucepan or a Dutch oven with a lid, heat the remaining 3 tablespoons of oil over medium-high heat. Brown the lamb on all sides and remove to a plate. Add the peppers, onion, chiles, and oregano and sauté until soft, about 3 minutes. Add the wine and broth, and bring to a simmer. Return the lamb to the pan and add the lime. Bring to a simmer, cover, and cook 1 hour, or until the lamb is very tender.

Remove the lime pieces and stir in the bananas. Cook for 5 minutes, stirring, until the mixture thickens. Stir in the cilantro and season to taste with more salt and pepper, if necessary.

Shrimp, Banana, and Kumquat Curry

Simmering the spices creates a wonderful brown butter–flavored sauce. Although kumquats are seasonal in most places, this citrusy, sweet banana curry is worth waiting for. Serve it with saffron rice flavored with raisins and almonds.

Makes 4 servings

2 tablespoons butter

³/₄ teaspoon curry powder

³/₄ teaspoon ground coriander

Pinch of cayenne

1¹/₄ cups heavy cream

6 finger bananas, cut into ¹/₄-inch-
  thick slices

6 kumquats, finely chopped

1¹/₄ pounds large shrimp, peeled
  and deveined

Salt

Freshly milled black pepper

Fresh cilantro

Heat the butter in a large skillet over medium heat. Add the curry, coriander, and cayenne and cook about 2 minutes, stirring, until the spices are fragrant and the butter has browned (do not burn). Pour in the cream, ³/₄ cup water, bananas, and kumquats and continue to stir until the mixture begins to thicken, about 3 minutes. Add the shrimp and cook until they turn pink and are just cooked through, about 2 to 3 minutes. Season to taste with salt and pepper, and garnish with cilantro.

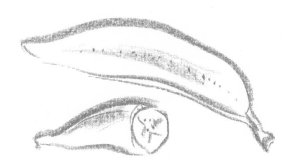

Grilled Ginger Shrimp with Banana Caper Relish

Grilled spicy shrimp and this tangy-sweet banana relish will make you think of a thatched-roof restaurant in the West Indies. This is a great summer party dish that I like to serve with white rice tossed with sliced scallions. If you're not making it during grilling season, you can broil the skewered shrimp in the oven.

Makes 4 servings

1/4 cup apricot preserves

1 tablespoon finely minced gingerroot

1 tablespoon soy sauce

3 tablespoons rice wine vinegar

1 tablespoon extra-hot habañero or other Caribbean-style pepper sauce

1 1/2 pounds large shrimp, shelled and deveined

Banana Caper Relish (recipe follows)

6 to 8 long wooden or metal skewers

Lime wedges

Combine the preserves, gingerroot, soy sauce, vinegar, and 1/4 cup water in a small saucepan. Bring to a boil, then lower the heat and simmer the mixture, stirring occasionally, 5 minutes. Remove from the heat and stir in the habañero sauce; allow to cool to room temperature. Place the shrimp in a bowl and pour the cooled marinade over the shrimp. Cover tightly with plastic wrap and refrigerate at least 2 hours, or overnight.

Just before grilling the shrimp, make the relish and set it aside. If using wooden skewers, soak them in water 30 minutes. Preheat the grill (or broiler, if using) to medium-high. Thread 4 to 5 shrimp on each skewer. Grill or broil the shrimp about 2 minutes per side, or until the shrimp turns pink and is cooked through. Arrange on plates with the relish, lime wedges, and rice, if desired.

Banana Caper Relish

The relish is very tasty on its own—or you can also serve it with grilled steak or chicken.

Makes about 2 cups

3 tablespoons extra virgin olive oil

1 medium red onion, thinly sliced

3 garlic cloves, minced

4 firm-ripe bananas, quartered lengthwise and diced

1/4 cup drained capers

2 tablespoons fresh lime juice

1 tablespoon rice wine vinegar

Salt

Freshly milled black pepper

2 tablespoons minced fresh parsley

Heat the oil in a large skillet over medium heat and cook the onion and garlic until soft. Add the bananas, capers, lime juice, and vinegar and cook 2 to 3 minutes, until bananas are just heated through. Remove from the heat and season to taste with salt and pepper. Stir in the parsley and keep relish warm until serving.

Jerk Fried Flounder with Banana-Kiwi Salsa

Gingery tropical fruit salsa cools the mild heat of this fish. If desired, you could even make fish fingers and serve this as an appetizer. Double the recipe for the spice rub and keep it on hand to rub on steak or for hot and spicy fried chicken.

Makes 4 servings

Banana-Kiwi Salsa (recipe follows)

Jerk Spice Rub:
1 teaspoon kosher salt
$1/2$ teaspoon freshly milled black pepper
2 teaspoons chile powder
2 teaspoons garlic salt
2 teaspoons red pepper flakes
2 teaspoons dried oregano
2 teaspoons dried thyme
1 teaspoon nutmeg
1 teaspoon ground cinnamon

1 teaspoon ground allspice
$1/2$ teaspoon ground cumin
2 teaspoons brown sugar

$1/2$ cup all-purpose flour
4 tablespoons vegetable oil
1 tablespoon butter
$1/2$ cup milk
4 (6-ounce) fillets flounder, halibut, cod, or other firm, white-fleshed fish
Lemon wedges

Combine the spice-rub ingredients in a spice grinder or blender and pulse a few times to blend. (Keep the remaining spice mixture in a small jar in a cool, dark place.) Add 2 tablespoons of the spice rub to the flour on a plate and stir to blend.

Heat 2 tablespoons of the oil and the butter in a large skillet over medium-high heat. Place the milk in a shallow bowl and dip the fish fillets first in milk, then in the seasoned flour, coating well. Cook on both sides until golden brown and crisp (about 6 to 8 minutes total cooking time), adding more oil if necessary. Transfer to plates, and spoon a dollop or two of banana-kiwi salsa alongside the fish and lemon wedges.

Banana-Kiwi Salsa

A fresh-tasting salsa that's great with any grilled meat or fish.

Makes 2 cups

$1/2$ cup diced firm-ripe banana

1 cup diced fresh (or unsweetened canned) pineapple

1 kiwi, peeled and diced

$1/4$ cup minced red onion

1 tablespoon minced gingerroot

2 tablespoons minced cilantro

1 tablespoon fresh lemon juice

$1/4$ teaspoon cayenne pepper

Combine ingredients in a bowl and chill until ready to serve.

Sea Bass Baked in Banana Leaf

Baking fish in a banana leaf is a traditional cooking method in many Asian countries. In addition to lending a delicate flavor to fish and preserving its juices, it's a lovely presentation for guests to unwrap at the dinner table. Serve this with an aromatic rice such as basmati or jasmine.

Makes 4 servings

Coconut marinade:

1 cup unsweetened, canned coconut milk or half-and-half, stir well

$^1/_4$ cup chopped red bell pepper

4 garlic cloves, chopped

1 jalapeño chile, seeded and coarsely chopped

$^1/_4$ cup fresh basil

2 teaspoons grated lime peel

Juice of 1 lime

$^1/_4$ teaspoon ground turmeric

1 teaspoon sugar

1 teaspoon salt

4 (6-ounce) thick, sea bass fillets or other firm white-fleshed fish

4 (12-inch) banana leaf squares*

Lime wedges

In a food processor or blender, combine the marinade ingredients and purée until smooth. Trim the narrow tail piece from the fillets to make them more of a rectangular shape. Place the fillets in a shallow baking dish and pour the marinade over them. Cover with plastic wrap and refrigerate for at least 30 minutes.

Preheat the oven to 425°F. Lift the fillets and allow the excess marinade to drip off (but do not scrape or shake too much of it off). Place a fillet in the center of each banana leaf. Fold the banana leaf around the fish—as you would wrap a present—into a neat package. Secure the package with one or two sturdy wooden toothpicks or half a wooden skewer, being careful to pierce the banana leaf only and not the fish inside.

Place the packets, seam side up, on a large baking sheet lightly sprayed with vegetable oil. Bake 12 to 15 minutes (for a $^3/_4$- or 1-inch-thick fillet), or until an instant-read thermometer reads 125°F when inserted into the center of the packet. Be careful not to overbake the fish. Alternately, you can grill the fish packages over medium-hot heat or coals, about 4 minutes each side.

Transfer the packets to plates, seam side up, and serve with lime wedges and rice. Allow each diner to open the packet at the table.

Simple Tomato and Herb Variation

Instead of marinating the fish fillets, simply place the raw fish in the center of the banana leaf. Place three $\frac{1}{4}$-inch-thick slices of tomato on top of each fillet, sprinkle with salt and freshly milled black pepper, and top with 2 or 3 large basil leaves or flat-leaf parsley sprigs. Drizzle with olive oil. Fold, seal, and bake the fillets as explained above.

*See page 14 for instructions on preparing banana leaves for cooking.

Red Snapper with Pecan-Banana Butter

Red bananas and pecans meld together in this simple sauce. Catfish, haddock, or any other firm white-fleshed fish will work equally well. Serve this simple supper dish with roasted potatoes, a green salad, and ice-cold white wine.

Makes 4 servings

$1/2$ cup all-purpose flour

2 teaspoons hot paprika

$1/4$ teaspoon dried thyme

$1/2$ teaspoon salt

$1/2$ cup milk

3 tablespoons peanut or canola oil

4 (6-ounce) red snapper fillets, or other firm white-fleshed fish

4 tablespoons butter

$1/3$ cup chopped pecans

$1/4$ teaspoon freshly grated nutmeg

Pinch of salt

2 ripe red bananas (or 1 large firm-ripe banana), diced

2 tablespoons fresh lime juice

2 tablespoons minced fresh cilantro or parsley

Stir together the flour, paprika, thyme, and salt on a large plate. Pour the milk into a shallow bowl. Heat the oil in a large skillet over medium heat until hot but not smoking.

Dip the fish fillets in the milk and then in the seasoned flour. Immediately place in the hot oil. Cook the fillets, in batches if necessary, until nicely browned on the bottom. Turn fillets and brown on the other side (about 4 minutes on each side for $3/4$- to 1-inch fillets). Remove to a platter and keep warm.

Drain off the cooking oil and wipe out the skillet with a paper towel. Heat the butter over medium heat and add the pecans, nutmeg, and salt. Cook, stirring, until the pecans are lightly browned, about 3 minutes. Add the bananas and cook, stirring, about 1 minute or until just heated through. Remove from the heat and stir in the lime juice and cilantro. Place the fillets on plates, spoon some of the sauce over each, and serve immediately.

Thai Spiced Vegetable Curry

This is a pleasantly spicy and creamy coconut-milk–based curry, flavored with chile, ginger, and lemongrass. Green bananas soften the contrasting flavors. Serve this hearty vegetarian dish with fragrant jasmine rice or another long-grain white rice such as American basmati.

Makes 4 to 6 servings

2 tablespoons vegetable oil

1 medium onion, chopped

1 red bell pepper, seeded and diced

2 cloves garlic, minced

2 green serrano chiles, seeded and minced

2 teaspoons minced gingerroot

3 cups unsweetened, canned coconut milk, stir well

$1/2$ cup vegetable or chicken broth plus $1/4$ cup water

1 (2-inch) cinnamon stick

1 (2-inch) stalk lemongrass, lightly pounded with a mallet or crushed

$1/2$ teaspoon ground turmeric

$1/4$ teaspoon curry powder

1 small ($1/2$-pound) eggplant, cut into $3/4$-inch cubes and steamed until tender

2 green bananas, sliced lengthwise and cut into $1/2$-inch pieces

1 medium tomato, seeded and chopped

$1/2$ cup trimmed green beans, cut into 1-inch pieces and steamed until tender

$1/2$ cup frozen petite peas

Salt

2 tablespoons fresh lime juice

6 large basil leaves, slivered

In a large, deep saucepan or wok, heat the oil over medium-high heat. Stir-fry the onion, bell pepper, garlic, chile, and gingerroot until soft. Add 2 cups of the coconut milk, the broth, cinnamon stick, lemongrass, turmeric, and curry powder. Bring to a boil; reduce the heat and simmer 10 minutes. Add the eggplant, bananas, and tomato, and simmer 10 minutes, or until the bananas are just soft. Stir in the beans, peas, and the remaining 1 cup of coconut milk and simmer 5 minutes more. Remove the cinnamon and lemongrass. Taste and season the curry with salt; stir in the lime juice and basil. Serve the curry in shallow bowls with a scoop of rice.

Quimbombo

Okra Stew with Plantain Dumplings

I grew up in the South eating okra stew and never thought it could be improved upon until I discovered this spicy Cuban version spiked with lime juice, dried chiles, and oregano. Even better, it's topped with plantain dumplings as light as good Italian gnocchi. I call for fresh tomatoes, but during the winter months I would substitute about 2 cups stewed tomatoes.

Makes 4 to 6 servings

1½ pounds small okra (or frozen okra, thawed and drained)
4 tablespoons fresh lime juice
¼ cup olive oil
1 small dried red chile, crumbled
3 garlic cloves, minced
1 cup thinly sliced onion
1 cup chopped red bell pepper
2 medium tomatoes, seeded and chopped

1 tablespoon minced fresh oregano (or 2 teaspoons dried)
1 cup chicken or vegetable broth
Salt
Freshly milled black pepper

Plantain dumplings:
1½ ripe plantains (yellowish with dark streaks)
3 tablespoons all-purpose flour
1 tablespoon butter

Remove the okra stems and slice into 1-inch pieces. Place in a bowl and cover with cold water and 3 tablespoons of the lime juice. Soak for 30 minutes to remove most of the viscous okra juice. Drain and pat dry with paper towels. You should have a little over 4 cups of okra.

While the okra is soaking, cut off the tips of the plantains and cut into 2-inch pieces. Cook in boiling salted water 10 to 20 minutes, or until the plantain is tender when pierced with a sharp knife. Drain, reserving ¼ cup of the liquid, and let sit until cool enough to handle. Mash plantains with cooking liquid or place in the food processor and purée. Add the flour and butter. The dough will be somewhat sticky. Wet your hands and form ping-pong-size-balls, about 1 inch in diameter. Cover with plastic wrap and set aside. (You can make the dumplings ahead of time and refrigerate them.)

Heat the oil in a large skillet and add the chile, garlic, onion, and bell pepper. Sauté about 5 minutes, or until the onions are soft. Add the tomatoes and okra, and sauté 5 more minutes. Add the oregano, broth, and remaining tablespoon of lime juice and bring to a boil. Lower heat, cover, and simmer until okra is tender, about 10 minutes. Add salt and pepper to taste. (If stew seems dry, add more broth or water.) Just before serving, place the dumplings on top of the simmering stew, lightly dunking them in the cooking juices. Cover and cook 5 minutes, or until dumplings are just heated through.

Variation

Plantain dumplings in sage butter. Prepare the dumplings as described above and set aside before cooking. Heat 4 tablespoons of butter in a large skillet with 15 or so fresh sage leaves and cook until the butter turns lightly brown. Cook the dumplings in a large pot of boiling salted water, 2 to 3 minutes, or until they float to the top and are just cooked. Drain and toss with the sage butter and salt, freshly milled pepper, and grated Parmesan to taste.

Bananas
on the Side

Slipping on a Peel

After the Spanish-American War of 1898 and the popularization of the fruit,

Americans saw the comedy of the banana. Vaudevillians were taken by the

banana's phallic shape; other less risqué comedians used it in jokes such as

'Remember the banana; when it leaves the bunch it gets skinned' and "The only

time some fellows have a girl smile at them is when they slip on a banana peel."

Movies featuring slapstick comedians, like those of Mack Sennett and his famous

Keystone Cops, brought the lubricant properties of banana skins to new heights;

scenes of pompous fools sliding on peels brought down the house. That slickness

was so renowned that passengers brought several successful lawsuits against rail-

road companies for bodily injuries occasioned by slipping and falling on banana

skins.

—Alex Abella, *The Total Banana* (Harcourt Brace Jovanovich, 1979)

Baked Sweet Potatoes and Plantains

Just a little maple syrup enhances the natural sweetness of the potatoes and ripe plantains. This dish pairs nicely with roast lamb or pork dishes.

Makes 4 to 6 servings

3 medium sweet potatoes

3 very ripe, black-skinned plantains

Grated zest and juice of 1 large navel orange

4 tablespoons butter, melted

3 tablespoons maple syrup

$^1/_4$ teaspoon pure vanilla extract

1 tablespoon grated gingerroot

$^1/_2$ teaspoon ground nutmeg

Pinch of salt

8 ginger snaps, crushed

Scrub potatoes and cut off root ends. Place in a large pot of salted water, cover, and bring to a boil. Boil about 35 minutes, or until just tender. Remove from the water. Cut the plantains in half without peeling and boil in the same water 15 to 20 minutes, until tender. Remove from the water and let stand until cool enough to handle. Peel the potatoes and the plantains, and slice crosswise into $^1/_3$-inch-thick circles.

Preheat the oven to 375°F. Butter a 2-quart casserole or baking dish. Layer sweet potatoes and plantains. Stir together the orange juice, zest, 2 tablespoons of the butter, the maple syrup, vanilla, ginger, nutmeg, and salt. Drizzle over the potatoes and plantains. Mix the ginger snaps with the remaining 2 tablespoons of butter and scatter over the top. Bake 20 minutes, or until the top is lightly browned and the casserole is simmering hot.

Indian Spiced Pilaf with Green Bananas

This is a very nice rice dish that also makes a hearty vegetarian dinner with the addition of sautéed tofu cubes or cooked chickpeas.

Makes 4 servings

2 tablespoons butter, ghee, or
   vegetable oil
2 teaspoons black mustard seeds
1 medium yellow onion, chopped
1 small green chile, seeded and minced
1 teaspoon Madras (hot) curry powder
1 cup long-grain white rice, such as
   basmati

1 green banana, quartered and
   diced (or half a yellow plantain)
2 cups chicken or vegetable broth
Salt
Freshly milled black pepper
2 tablespoons chopped fresh
   cilantro, or to taste
3 tablespoons sliced almonds, toasted

Heat the butter in a medium saucepan over medium heat. Add the mustard seeds and stir until they begin to pop. Add the onion, chile, and curry powder and cook, stirring, until the onions are soft. Add the rice and banana and cook 1 minute, or until the rice just begins to turn golden.

Add the broth and bring to a boil. Cover and reduce heat to lowest setting; simmer 15 minutes. Remove from the heat and, with the lid on, allow the rice to steam for 15 minutes more. Add salt and pepper to taste. Transfer to a serving bowl and top with cilantro and almonds.

Crusty Baked Green Bananas

Choose green-tipped, yellow bananas that are about two days from being ripe enough to use on your morning cereal. Crusty baked, barely sweet bananas are a nice switch from roasted potatoes and are good paired with roast chicken or grilled steak. You can also make this dish using finger bananas, figuring two per person. This recipe is based on one from Gourmet magazine.

Makes 4 servings

4 tablespoons butter, melted

$1/4$ cup plus 1 tablespoon fresh lime juice

$1/2$ teaspoon salt

Pinch of freshly milled pepper

$1/2$ cup finely grated Parmesan cheese

$1/2$ cup dried bread crumbs

$1/2$ teaspoon paprika

4 green-tipped yellow bananas

Preheat the oven to 375°F. Stir together the butter, lime juice, salt, and pepper in a shallow bowl. Combine the Parmesan, bread crumbs, and paprika on a large plate.

Peel the bananas and slice them in half, then halve them lengthwise so that each banana makes 4 pieces. Coat banana pieces on all sides in the butter-lime mixture, then coat with the Parmesan crumbs. Arrange the banana pieces in a single layer in a buttered, shallow baking pan, approximately 9 x 13 inches. Bake 25 minutes, or until the bananas turn golden brown and crusty. Drizzle with the remaining butter-lime mixture before serving.

Maduros with Spicy Black Beans and Yellow Rice

Wander into any Hispanic cafe and you're likely to be offered beans and rice and fried sweet plantains (or tostones), with your dinner entrée. It's the holy trinity of Latino food and a delicious meal all on its own.

Makes 4 to 6 Servings

Vegetable oil for frying

3 ripe, yellow- to black-skinned plantains

Kosher salt

In an electric skillet, deep fryer, or a large pot with a thermometer attached, heat 1½ inches of oil to 375°F.

With a sharp knife, trim the ends from the plantains and cut them in half crosswise. Cut a shallow slit through the skin inside the curve of each piece. Pry the skin away from the plantain with your fingers (see plantain peeling tips, page 13).

Cut the plantains into long, diagonal slices about ½-inch thick. Fry in batches 3 to 4 minutes, turning once, until plantains are golden. Using a slotted spatula or spoon, transfer to paper towels to drain briefly before salting. Maduros are best served immediately with beans and rice, if desired.

To reheat maduros, place on a baking sheet in a 350°F oven about 5 minutes, or until heated through.

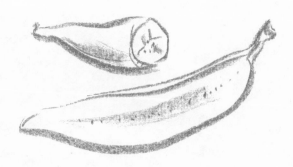

Spicy Black Beans

Makes 4 to 6 servings

½ pound (about 1¼ cups) dried
  black beans

2 tablespoons olive oil or bacon
  drippings

2 minced garlic cloves

1 medium onion, diced

1 serrano chile, seeded and chopped

Salt

Freshly milled black pepper

Rinse and pick over the beans. Place the beans in a medium saucepan and cover with 4 cups of water. Bring to a boil and cook 2 minutes. Remove from the heat and let stand, covered, for at least 1 hour. Drain and add 4 cups of fresh water. Return the beans to a boil, cover, and reduce to a simmer. Cook the beans until tender but still retaining their shape, about 1 hour (though some beans take longer). Drain the beans and keep them warm.

In a large saucepan, heat the oil over medium heat and add the garlic, onion, and chile. Saute until the onion is soft. Stir onion mixture into the cooked beans. Season to taste with salt and pepper.

Yellow Rice

Makes 4 to 6 servings

2 cups water

2 cups chicken broth (low sodium
  if using canned)

Large pinch of saffron threads,
  crumbled (or ¼ teaspoon
  ground turmeric)

½ teaspoon salt

2 cups long-grain white rice

1 tablespoon butter

Place the water, broth, saffron, and salt in a medium saucepan and bring to a boil. Add the rice and stir; reduce the heat to low and cover. Cook 20 to 25 minutes, until the rice is tender. Stir in the butter before serving.

Bananas à la Milanesa

Hopefully your fear of frying isn't so great that you would pass these up. In Brazil anything rolled in bread crumbs and fried is à la Milanesa, and bananas are wonderful prepared in this manner. These pair nicely with Spicy Black Beans and Yellow Rice (page 99).

Makes 4 servings

3 large eggs, beaten with
  1 tablespoon milk
1 cup dried bread crumbs
Salt
Vegetable oil for frying

8 to 10 ripe finger bananas
  (or 4 firm-ripe large bananas),
  peeled and left whole

Beat the eggs and milk in a shallow bowl, and place the bread crumbs and a pinch or two of salt on a plate. Heat 2½ to 3 inches of oil in an electric skillet, deep fryer, or a large pot with a thermometer attached to 350°F.

Dip each banana first in the egg, then coat evenly with the bread crumbs. Fry the bananas until they are golden brown on all sides, about 3 to 4 minutes. Serve hot.

Sautéed Spicy Plantains

You'll want very ripe plantains to make this spicy sweet dish, which is very popular throughout South America. Stir a little milk into the sour cream so you can easily drizzle it over the cooked plantains.

Makes 4 servings

2 very ripe, black-skinned plantains

1 tablespoon butter

1 tablespoon canola oil

1 jalapeño chile, seeded and thinly
  sliced

Salt

Freshly milled black pepper

$1/3$ cup sour cream, thinned
  with milk

Cut off the ends of the plantains and peel them. Cut in half crosswise, then again in half lengthwise to quarter them. Heat the butter and oil in a large skillet over medium heat. Sauté the plantains and chile, turning occasionally, until the plantains are nicely browned on all sides. Transfer to a serving dish, season with salt and pepper to taste, and drizzle with the sour cream.

Boiled Plantains

Boiled plantains with a bit of butter taste almost like cooked sweet potatoes, though they're more starchy in texture. The addition of melted cheese may strike you as odd, but it is an irresistible topping. You can also sprinkle the boiled plantains with cinnamon, cayenne, or even add a dollop of sour cream along with the butter—whatever strikes your fancy.

4 very ripe, black-skinned plantains
Butter
Salt

$^{1}/_{2}$ pound shredded fresh mozzarella cheese, optional

Cut off the ends of the plantains, slice them in half, and leave the skins on. Place them in a large pot of boiling water and cook, covered, 15 to 20 minutes, or until the plantains are tender. Remove with a slotted spoon. Peel and slice the pieces in half. Season with butter and salt to taste. If desired, sprinkle pieces with cheese and place under a broiler 1 to 2 minutes until hot and bubbly.

Variation

Roasted Plantain: Line a baking dish with foil and place the plantains, skins on, in the dish. Prick the skins with a sharp knife a few times to allow the steam to escape. Bake at 350°F about 35 minutes, or until the plantains are soft and the flesh cooked through. Alternately, prick the skins, and place the plantains in a glass dish, and microwave on high power for 5 minutes, turning occasionally to cook evenly. Peel and slice the pieces in half. Season with butter and salt to taste. If desired, sprinkle pieces with cheese and place under a broiler 1 to 2 minutes until hot and bubbly.

Squash and Plantain Purée

1 small (about 1^1/$_2$ pounds) acorn
   or butternut squash

8 garlic cloves, skins on

2 ripe, black-skinned plantains,
   peeled and chopped

2^1/$_2$ cups chicken broth

2 tablespoons butter

^{1}/$_2$ cup sour cream

2 teaspoons fresh thyme, or
   ^{1}/$_2$ teaspoon dried

Salt

Freshly milled black pepper

Early in the day, heat the oven to 400°F and cut the squash in half lengthwise; scoop out the seeds and discard. Line a baking sheet with aluminum foil and lightly spray it with vegetable oil. Place the squash, cut side down, on the baking sheet and place the garlic inside the hollowed out center. Bake 30 to 40 minutes, or until the squash is very soft. Cool and then scoop out the squash flesh with a spoon. Squeeze the pulp from the garlic skins and add to the squash. Set aside.

Place the plantains and 2 cups of the broth in a medium saucepan and bring to a boil. Reduce the heat and simmer 15 minutes, or until the plantains are soft and tender and most of the broth has been absorbed. Place the plantains in the bowl of a food processor along with the squash, garlic, butter, sour cream, thyme, and salt and pepper to taste. Process until the mixture becomes a thick purée. Return to the pan and add more broth to bring to the desired consistency. Cook over medium-low heat until just heated through. Drizzle with more butter, if desired.

Grilled Bananas

Searing these molasses-basted bananas on the grill makes them extra flavorful and a sweet contrast to spicy chicken or beef. Remove the peel before eating.

Makes 4 to 6 servings

4 to 6 firm-ripe bananas

3 tablespoons molasses
  (not blackstrap)

2 tablespoons butter

1 tablespoon fresh lime juice

Split the bananas lengthwise, leaving the peel intact. Lightly spray the grill with vegetable oil and preheat to medium-high heat (or prepare charcoal). Heat the molasses, butter, and lime juice in a small saucepan until the butter is melted. Brush the bananas with the molasses mixture and grill on both sides 2 to 3 minutes, or until the cut side is golden brown. Serve hot.

Do Monkeys Like Bananas?

Monkeys, chimpanzees, gorillas, and other primates have pretty diverse diets but they do seem to enjoy bananas, particularly when they come across a ripe bunch in the wild, according to nutrition experts at the Bronx Zoo. African chimpanzees are quite skilled and use both their feet and hands to hold and peel ripe fruit. Peels and unripe fruit that do not please their palate are tossed to the jungle floor, becoming dinner for insects and other small animals.

Many tropical creatures seem to love bananas. The macaw, a long-tailed parrot from Central and South America uses its sharp claws to grip the fruit as it rips it from the stem. *Caligo eurilochus,* the owl butterfly that lives in the same jungles, prefers rotten bananas and can actually become drunk from the fermented fruit juices.

Plantain, Apple, and Bacon Stuffing

This stuffing proves that everything goes better with bacon. Plantains and apples lend fruit overtones, and walnuts a bit of crunch. Hot sausage can be used in place of the bacon. Try this as a moist and flavorful stuffing for your Thanksgiving bird. It is even better with homemade gravy—spike it with sherry—drizzled over it.

Makes about 12 cups, or 12 to 16 servings

$1/2$ pound slab bacon

2 tablespoons butter

2 medium onions, chopped

4 garlic cloves, minced

3 celery ribs and heart with leaves, chopped

2 Granny Smith or other tart apples, cored and diced

3 ripe, black-skinned plantains, peeled and diced

2 tablespoons finely slivered fresh sage (or 1 tablespoon dried, crumbled sage)

2 teaspoons fresh thyme

1 (16-ounce) package cornbread stuffing (or 6 cups cornbread crumbs)

3 cups white bread cubes, dried overnight or toasted in the oven

$1/3$ cup minced fresh parsley

1 cup walnut pieces, coarsely chopped and toasted

2 large eggs

1 cup half-and-half

2 tablespoons dry sherry or cognac

1 teaspoon salt

$1/2$ teaspoon freshly milled black pepper

$1/2$ to $3/4$ cup chicken or turkey broth

Cut away the tough rind from the underside of the bacon. Cut into $1/2$-inch pieces, about $1/4$-inch thick. In a large skillet, cook the bacon until browned on all sides. Transfer to a plate lined with paper towels and set aside. You should have about $1/3$ cup of bacon drippings; if not, add olive oil to make $1/3$ cup.

Heat the drippings and the butter in the skillet over medium heat. Add the onions, garlic, celery, apples, and plantains and cook, stirring, until the onions are soft. Add the sage and thyme, and cook 1 to 2 minutes more, until fragrant.

Combine the stuffing, bread cubes, parsley, and walnuts in a large bowl. Add the cooked onion mixture and the bacon. Beat together the eggs, half-and-half, sherry, salt, and pepper. Pour over the bread mixture and toss well to combine the ingredients. Add just enough broth to evenly moisten the stuffing (it should not be soggy). Use to stuff a turkey, or place in a large, buttered baking dish. Cover with foil and bake at 350°F for 30 minutes. Remove the foil and bake 5 minutes longer, or until the top is lightly browned and crusty.

Green Banana and Potato Salad

One of my friends describes this salad as "shockingly good," and I couldn't agree more. It has become my favorite picnic potato salad. It is based on a traditional Puerto Rican dish, guineos y papas, *which is usually served with yellow rice and found on the buffet table at large social gatherings. The salad is best eaten within a day or so because the bananas tend to darken.*

Makes 8 to 10 servings

2$^1/_2$ pounds red-skinned or Yukon Gold potatoes, peeled and cut into 1-inch cubes

3 pounds greenish-yellow bananas (about 7 or 8 bananas), sliced into 1-inch pieces

2 medium onions, sliced

$^1/_2$ cup Spanish capers, drained

1 cup pimento-stuffed Spanish olives, halved

$^3/_4$ cup extra virgin olive oil

$^1/_2$ cup white vinegar

1 tablespoon Dijon mustard

2$^1/_2$ teaspoons salt

1 teaspoon freshly milled black pepper

Cook the potatoes in boiling salted water until firm-tender, about 8 to 10 minutes. Add the bananas to the pot and boil 1 minute more. Drain. In a large serving bowl, layer the warm bananas and potatoes with the onions, capers, and olives. Whisk together the oil, vinegar, mustard, salt, and pepper, then pour the mixture over the salad. Cover with plastic wrap and refrigerate at least 2 hours.

Banana Breads

The Bananas

The bananas grow thick.

Now we go gather them.

The bananas grow thick,

Now they lie in our hands.

The bananas grow thick.

Now we pick the ripe ones.

The bananas grow thick,

See how they lie on the stem.

The bananas grow thick.

Our skirts are filled with them.

The bananas grow thick,

We tuck our skirts over our belts.

—Anonymous from the Chou Dynasty, 1112 B.C.–249 B.C.

Classic Banana Bread

This makes a pretty, round-topped loaf with lots of dark banana specks. If desired, you can fold one cup of coarsely chopped, toasted walnuts or pecans into the batter just before pouring it into the loaf pan. Serve a slice with apricot preserves for tea, or toast it for breakfast and spread with butter and honey.

Makes one 9 x 5 x 3-inch loaf, or 18 muffins

2^1/$_2$ cups all-purpose flour

2 teaspoons baking powder

^{1}/$_2$ teaspoon baking soda

^{1}/$_4$ teaspoon salt

1^1/$_2$ cups mashed very ripe banana (about 4 bananas)

^{1}/$_4$ cup buttermilk or milk

^{1}/$_2$ cup (1 stick) unsalted butter

^{2}/$_3$ cup sugar

2 large eggs

2 teaspoons pure vanilla extract

Preheat the oven to 350°F. Grease and flour a 9 x 5 x 3-inch loaf pan. Sift together the flour, baking powder, baking soda, and salt. Set aside. Mix together the bananas and buttermilk.

Beat the butter and sugar in a large bowl with an electric mixer until very light and fluffy. Add the eggs and vanilla and beat to incorporate. Add the flour mixture alternately with the banana mixture, mixing only until the ingredients are just blended. Spoon the batter into the prepared pan. Bake 1 hour and 10 minutes (30 to 35 minutes for muffins), or until a wooden skewer inserted in the center comes out clean. Cool in the pan 10 minutes, then turn out onto a cake rack to cool completely.

Chocolate-Chunk Banana Bread

I made dozens of loaves of this rum-spiked, chocolate-studded banana bread one year for holiday presents, and they were a tremendous hit. For elegant gift-giving, place each one in a clear cellophane bag and tie with a pretty silver ribbon.

Makes one 9 x 5 x 3-inch loaf, or 15 muffins

^{2}/3 cup granulated sugar

^{1}/2 cup (1 stick) unsalted butter, softened

2 large eggs

2^1/2 cups plus 2 tablespoons cake flour

2 teaspoons baking powder

^{1}/4 teaspoon salt

1 teaspoon ground cinnamon

^{1}/2 teaspoon ground allspice

1 cup mashed ripe banana (about 2^1/2 bananas)

^{1}/3 cup strong coffee, cold

1 teaspoon pure vanilla extract

1 cup semisweet chocolate chunks or large chips

2 to 3 tablespoons dark or spiced rum

Confectioners' sugar for dusting

Preheat the oven to 350°F. Grease the bottom of a 9 x 5 x 3-inch loaf pan, line it with wax paper, and grease and flour the bottom and sides.

Beat the sugar and butter in a large bowl with an electric mixer until very light and fluffy. Add the eggs, one at a time, beating until light. Stir together the flour, baking powder, salt, cinnamon, and allspice. Combine the banana, coffee, and vanilla. With the mixer on the lowest setting, add the dry ingredients alternately with the banana mixture in three parts until just incorporated. Using a rubber spatula, fold in the chocolate.

Spoon the batter into the prepared pan and bake 55 minutes to 1 hour (25 to 30 minutes for muffins), or until a wooden skewer inserted in the center comes out clean. Cool in the pan 10 minutes, then turn out onto a rack. Remove the wax paper and drizzle the bottom with a little rum. Turn it right side up and drizzle the top with rum; cool completely. Before slicing, sprinkle the top of the loaf with confectioners' sugar.

Banana-Carrot Loaf

What could be better than a carrot cake with the sweet taste of bananas? Its moist, rich flavor is actually improved by serving it the day after it is baked; and it is delicious with softened-cream cheese. Or you can divide the batter to make muffins and top them with Cream Cheese Frosting (page 137), making luscious little cupcakes.

Makes one 9 x 5 x 3-inch loaf, or 18 muffins

$1/2$ cup canola oil

$1/2$ cup packed dark brown sugar

2 large eggs

$1/2$ cup mashed ripe banana
   (about $1^1/4$ bananas)

2 cups all-purpose flour

1 teaspoon baking soda

$1/4$ teaspoon salt

1 teaspoon ground cinnamon

$1/2$ teaspoon ground nutmeg

1 cup finely grated carrot

Half a Granny Smith apple, cored
   and finely diced

$1/2$ cup chopped pecans, toasted

Preheat the oven to 350°F. Grease and flour a 9 x 5 x 3-inch loaf pan.

Place the oil, brown sugar, eggs, and banana in a large mixing bowl and beat well with an electric mixer. Stir together the flour, baking soda, salt, cinnamon, and nutmeg. With a mixer on the lowest speed, gradually add the dry ingredients to the egg mixture. Using a rubber spatula, fold in the carrot, apple, and pecans and spoon into prepared pan. Bake 55 minutes (25 to 30 minutes for muffins), or until a wooden skewer inserted in the center comes out clean. Cool in the pan 10 minutes, then turn out onto a rack to cool completely.

Whole Wheat Raisin-Banana Bread

This is a wholesome-tasting, barely sweet banana bread that freezes well. It makes a firm, rounded loaf that you can slice thinly and spread with cream cheese to make lovely tea sandwiches.

Makes one 8$^{1}/_{2}$ x 4$^{1}/_{2}$ x 2$^{3}/_{4}$-inch loaf, or 12 muffins

1 cup dark raisins

1 cup all-purpose flour

$^{3}/_{4}$ cup whole wheat flour

2 teaspoons baking powder

$^{1}/_{2}$ teaspoon baking soda

$^{1}/_{2}$ teaspoon salt

1$^{1}/_{2}$ teaspoons ground cinnamon

1 cup mashed very ripe banana

   (about 2$^{1}/_{2}$ bananas)

3 tablespoons milk

6 tablespoons unsalted butter, softened

$^{1}/_{3}$ cup packed light brown sugar

2 large eggs

1 teaspoon pure vanilla extract

Preheat the oven to 375°F. Grease and flour an 8½ x 4½ x 2¾-inch loaf pan.

Place the raisins in a small bowl and toss with 1 tablespoon of the all-purpose flour. Stir together the remaining all-purpose flour, the whole wheat flour, baking powder, baking soda, salt, and cinnamon. Mix together the banana and milk, and set aside.

Beat the butter and brown sugar in a large bowl with an electric mixer until light and fluffy. Beat in the eggs, one at a time, beating well after each addition; stir in the vanilla. Fold in the flour and banana mixtures using a large rubber spatula until just blended. Then fold in the raisins (do not overmix). Spoon the batter into the prepared pan. Bake the loaf 45 to 55 minutes (18 to 20 minutes for muffins), or until a wooden skewer inserted in the center of the loaf comes out clean. Cool on a rack 10 minutes. Run a butter knife around the edges, then remove from the pan and place on a rack to finish cooling.

Banana Cream Rinse

*I*nstead of conditioner, actress Catherine Zeta-Jones likes to mash whole bananas into her brunette tresses to make them shine, according to a recent article in *Allure* magazine. Bananas will also make your hair smell, so remember to wash them out thoroughly before you go out on a date.

What to do with banana peels?

*S*ome gardeners like to bury a banana peel in the dirt next to their potassium-loving rose bushes. You can also use them to make an all-natural mosquito trap: place two or three peels in a gallon of water along with a cup each of vinegar and sugar, and hang it from a tree.

African Peanut Cake

To make this cake (and most all of the banana breads), I use black-skinned, soft fruit that is so ripe you wouldn't think it was edible, but it gives the bread the desired intense banana flavor. Use skinned cocktail peanuts that come in a can rather than dry-roasted nuts. Like other banana breads this one also tastes best the second day.

Makes one 9 x 5 x 3-inch loaf, or 15 muffins

2 cups all-purpose flour

2 teaspoons baking powder

$1/4$ teaspoon baking soda

$1/4$ teaspoon salt

1 teaspoon freshly grated nutmeg

$1/2$ teaspoon ground mace

$1/2$ cup (1 stick) unsalted butter, softened

$3/4$ cup packed dark brown sugar

2 large eggs

$1^1/2$ teaspoons pure vanilla extract

2 cups mashed very ripe banana (about 6 bananas)

1 cup chopped salted peanuts

Confectioners' sugar for dusting

Preheat the oven to 350°F. Grease the bottom of a 9 x 5 x 3-inch loaf pan, line it with wax paper, and grease and flour the bottom and sides.

Stir together the flour, baking powder, baking soda, salt, nutmeg, and mace in a bowl. Cream the butter and brown sugar in a large bowl with an electric mixer until light and fluffy. Add the eggs, one at a time, beating well to incorporate; stir in the vanilla. Add the dry ingredients alternately with the mashed banana until just blended. Fold in $1/2$ cup of the peanuts with a rubber spatula.

Spoon the batter into the prepared pan and sprinkle the top evenly with the remaining nuts. Bake 55 to 60 minutes (25 to 30 minutes for muffins), or until a wooden skewer inserted in the center of the cake comes out clean. Cool in the pan 10 minutes, then invert on a rack. Remove the wax paper and turn the loaf right side up to cool completely. Lightly dust the top with confectioners' sugar before slicing.

Low-fat Banana-Blueberry Muffins

This and the following recipes are exceptionally good and just happen to be low in fat. Like applesauce, banana purée is an excellent fat replacer since it adds moisture and a sweet, tender texture to baked goods.

Makes 12 muffins or one 8¹/₂ x 4¹/₂ x 2³/₄-inch loaf

2¹/₄ cups all-purpose flour

1 teaspoon baking powder

1 teaspoon baking soda

¹/₂ teaspoon salt

¹/₃ cup packed light brown sugar, plus more for sprinkling tops

¹/₂ cup yogurt mixed with ¹/₄ cup milk

¹/₂ cup mashed very ripe banana (about 1¹/₄ bananas)

1 large egg

2 tablespoons butter, melted

1 teaspoon finely grated lemon zest

1 cup fresh blueberries, rinsed and picked over

Preheat the oven to 375°F. Lightly coat a 12-cup muffin tin with vegetable cooking spray or line it with paper baking cups.

Stir together the flour, baking powder, baking soda, and salt in a large bowl. In another bowl, whisk together the brown sugar, yogurt, banana, egg, butter, and lemon zest. Pour it into the dry ingredients and stir until just blended. Fold in the blueberries with a rubber spatula (be careful not to overmix the batter as it will cause the muffins to become heavy).

Spoon the batter into the paper-lined muffin cups and sprinkle a little brown sugar on the tops. Bake 18 to 20 minutes (45 to 50 minutes for a loaf), or until the muffins are firm to the touch and golden brown on top. Cool in the pan 5 minutes before turning out onto a rack to cool completely. Serve warm or at room temperature.

Low-fat Banana Bran Muffins

This is a light bran muffin with a subtle molasses flavor. Serve the muffins immediately and freeze the rest to keep them fresh. Warm them in a toaster oven before serving with apple butter or jam.

Makes 12 muffins, or one 8^1/$_2$ x 4^1/$_2$ x 2^3/$_4$-inch loaf

^{2}/$_3$ cup buttermilk

1 cup all-bran cereal (not bran flakes)

1^1/$_4$ cups all-purpose flour

2 teaspoons baking powder

^{1}/$_2$ teaspoon baking soda

^{1}/$_2$ teaspoon salt

^{1}/$_2$ teaspoon ground cinnamon

1 cup mashed very ripe banana

   (about 2^1/$_2$ bananas)

2 tablespoons vegetable oil

1 large egg

^{1}/$_3$ cup molasses

^{1}/$_4$ cup sugar

^{1}/$_3$ cup applesauce

^{1}/$_2$ cup chopped dates tossed in

   1 tablespoon flour

Preheat the oven to 375°F. Lightly coat a 12-cup muffin tin with vegetable cooking spray, or line it with paper baking cups.

Place the buttermilk and cereal in a small bowl and allow to stand 15 minutes. In a separate bowl, stir together the flour, baking powder, baking soda, salt, and cinnamon. In a larger bowl, blend together the banana, oil, egg, molasses, sugar, and applesauce. Add the buttermilk mixture and the flour mixture, stirring until well blended. Fold in the dates using a rubber spatula.

Spoon the batter into the muffin cups until they are three-quarters full. Bake 20 to 25 minutes, until muffins are well-risen and firm to the touch (55 minutes for a loaf).

Morning Glory Muffins

Orange zest and tart apricots give a bright sunny flavor to these moist, light muffins. Serve them warm with an orange-flavored butter and farm-stand honey.

Makes 18 muffins, or one 9 x 5 x 3-inch loaf pan

1 cup plus 2 tablespoons old-fashioned oats

1 cup buttermilk

2 tablespoons orange juice

1 teaspoon pure vanilla extract

1 tablespoon grated orange zest

1 ripe banana, diced

$1/3$ cup sweetened, shredded coconut

$1 1/4$ cups all-purpose flour

3 teaspoons baking powder

$1/2$ teaspoon baking soda

$1/2$ teaspoon salt

1 teaspoon ground cinnamon

1 teaspoon ground mace

1 large egg

$3/4$ cup packed light brown sugar

$1/4$ cup vegetable oil

$1/2$ cup finely chopped dried apricots

$1/4$ cup unsalted sunflower seeds, optional

Preheat the oven to 375°F. Grease a 12-cup muffin tin or line them with paper cups.

Combine the oats, buttermilk, juice, vanilla, zest, banana, and coconut in a bowl. In another bowl, stir together the flour, baking powder, baking soda, salt, cinnamon, and mace. Beat the egg, brown sugar, and oil in a large bowl with an electric mixer until thoroughly combined. Gradually add the oatmeal mixture until blended, then stir in the flour mixture until just combined (do not overmix). Fold in the apricots with a rubber spatula.

Spoon the batter into the muffin cups, until about two-thirds full. Sprinkle the tops with a few sunflower seeds, if using. Bake 18 minutes (50 minutes for a loaf), or until muffins are brown and raised, and firm to the touch. Cool muffins in the pan 5 minutes, then transfer to a rack to cool. Repeat steps with remaining batter.

Spicy Banana Gingerbread

Ultraripe bananas add another flavor dimension to this dark, very gingery bread and help keep it moist for days. While this gingerbread is great to snack on by itself, it also makes a homey dessert served with poached pear slices and a dab of crème fraîche. Or simply dust squares of the bread with confectioners' sugar and serve with tea. The secret to great gingerbread is using fresh spices, so if you can't remember the last time you replaced yours, it's probably a good idea to buy new ones.

Makes one 8-inch-square cake with nine 2 1/2-inch squares

1 (2-inch-long) piece gingerroot, coarsely chopped
6 tablespoons unsalted butter, softened
1/2 cup blackstrap molasses
3/4 cup packed dark brown sugar
1 large egg
1 1/2 cups all-purpose flour
2 teaspoons baking powder
1/2 teaspoon baking soda
1/2 teaspoon salt
2 teaspoons ground ginger
1 teaspoon ground cinnamon
1 teaspoon freshly grated nutmeg
1/2 cup mashed very ripe banana (about 1 1/4 bananas)
Confectioners' sugar for dusting

Preheat the oven to 350°F. Grease and flour an 8-inch-square baking pan.

Bring 1/2 cup of water and the gingerroot to a boil in a small saucepan. Remove from the heat, cover, and allow to steep 10 minutes. Strain and set aside; discard gingerroot.

Beat the butter, molasses, and brown sugar in a large bowl with an electric mixer until very creamy. Beat in the egg. In a separate bowl, stir together the flour, baking powder, baking soda, salt, ground ginger, cinnamon, and nutmeg. Stir together the banana and ginger water, and with the mixer on low speed, gradually add it to the butter mixture along with the dry ingredients, mixing until just blended.

Scrape the batter into the prepared pan and bake 35 to 40 minutes, or until a wooden skewer inserted in the center comes out clean. Place pan on a rack to cool completely. Sprinkle the top with confectioners' sugar, and slice into 9 even squares. Serve warm or at room temperature.

Banana Cakes

"Ripe, juicy cherries, pitted and mixed equally with banana

cubes, then sweetened, make a dessert my soul loves to recall."

—Martha McCullouch-Williams, 1913,
Dishes & Beverages of the Old South

Banana Pound Cake

Your pound cake will turn out beautifully if you follow the step-by-step directions for adding the dry and wet mixtures. For some reason, pound cakes always seem more moist and flavorful the next day, so I would make this the day before you plan to serve it. There's nothing like the pure, buttery flavor of this mildly flavored banana cake, and it is wonderful served plain; however, you can top it with fresh fruit or sorbet if desired. It also makes a nice base for ice cream and a dessert sauce—try coconut ice cream with the Banana-Raspberry Dessert Sauce (page 126), or pumpkin ice cream with Bittersweet Fudge Sauce (page 144).

Makes one 9 x 5 x 3-inch loaf

2 cups cake flour

$^3/_4$ teaspoon baking powder

$^1/_4$ teaspoon salt

$^1/_2$ teaspoon ground mace

$^1/_4$ teaspoon nutmeg (freshly grated)

4 large eggs, room temperature

$^1/_2$ cup plus 2 tablespoons mashed ripe banana (about $1^1/_4$ bananas)

$1^1/_2$ teaspoons pure vanilla extract

1 cup (2 sticks) unsalted butter, softened

1 cup sugar

Preheat the oven to 325°F. Grease the bottom of a 9 x 5 x 3-inch loaf pan and line with wax paper. Grease and flour the bottom and sides of the pan.

Sift together the flour, baking powder, salt, mace, and nutmeg. Sift again and set aside. Combine 1 egg, the banana, and vanilla in a small bowl and beat to incorporate. Set aside.

In a separate, larger bowl, beat the butter and sugar with an electric mixer until very light. Add the remaining 3 eggs, one at a time, beating well after each addition. Beat a third of the flour mixture into the butter-egg mixture. Add half the banana mixture, then repeat the addition of the flour and banana mixtures until combined (you should have made 5 additions).

Scrape the batter into the pan and bake about 1 hour, until the cake has risen, is golden brown on top, and a wooden skewer inserted in the center comes out clean. Cool the cake in the pan on a rack, then invert, remove the wax paper, and wrap tightly in plastic wrap so that the cake won't dry out. When you're ready to serve it, cut the cake with a serrated knife into 1-inch-thick slices.

Banana Layer Cake with Chocolate–Sour Cream Frosting

Bananas and chocolate are perfect together. Here, three delicate cake layers are stacked with creamy, rich chocolate–sour cream frosting in between—it's the banana lover's dream birthday cake. If desired, stir chocolate chips or your favorite nuts into the cake batter before baking.

1 cup mashed ripe banana
  (about 2 1/2 bananas)
1/4 cup sour cream
1 teaspoon pure vanilla extract
2 cups cake flour
1 teaspoon baking powder
1/2 teaspoon baking soda
1/4 teaspoon salt

1/2 cup (1 stick) unsalted butter,
  softened
1 1/4 cups sugar
3 large eggs
1/2 cup semisweet chocolate minichips
  or 1/2 cup chopped pecans, optional
Chocolate–Sour Cream Frosting
  (recipe follows)

Preheat the oven to 350°F. Butter and flour three 8-inch round cake pans. In a small bowl, mix together the banana, sour cream, and vanilla. In a separate bowl, stir together the flour, baking powder, baking soda, and salt. Set aside.

In a large bowl with an electric mixer, cream the butter and sugar until very light and fluffy, about 4 minutes. Add the eggs, one at a time, beating well after each addition. With the mixer on its lowest setting, add the flour and banana mixtures alternately, beginning and ending with the flour. Beat until just blended. Fold in the chocolate chips or pecans, if using.

Spoon the batter into the prepared pans, spreading evenly to the edges. Place the layers on two oven racks so that one is not directly above another. Bake 25 to 30 minutes, or until a wooden skewer inserted in the center comes out clean. Cool the pans on wire racks 10 minutes. Invert the cake layers onto wire racks, then turn right side up and cool completely.

Chocolate–Sour Cream Frosting

This is a rich, glossy frosting that stays soft and creamy. Pink birthday candles look especially pretty with the dark frosting.

18 ounces (1^1/$_2$ twelve-ounce packages, or 3 cups) semisweet chocolate morsels

1^1/$_2$ cups sour cream (don't use reduced calorie or nonfat)
Pinch of salt

Melt the chocolate in a small bowl over a pan of barely simmering water (or in a bowl in the microwave on medium power for approximately 2 minutes), until half melted. Remove from the heat and continue stirring until smooth. Add the sour cream and salt, and stir until thoroughly blended. Spread the frosting while it is still warm. Makes enough to frost a two- or three-layer 8- or 9-inch cake.

Banana Chiffon Cake with Banana-Raspberry Dessert Sauce

You can serve this light, springy sponge cake with raspberry sauce or split it into three layers, as I have here, and fill with whipped cream and bananas for a more sumptuous dessert. To make the cake, you'll need a 10-inch tube pan with a removable bottom (also called an angel food cake pan). You can borrow one from your mother, as I did, or purchase one at a cookware shop or a well-stocked hardware store.

Banana-Raspberry Dessert Sauce
(recipe follows)

2¹/₄ cups sifted cake flour

1¹/₄ cups granulated sugar

3 teaspoons baking powder

¹/₂ teaspoon salt

¹/₂ cup canola oil

6 large egg yolks

³/₄ cups mashed ripe banana
(about 1¹/₂ bananas)

Lemon juice

1 teaspoon pure vanilla extract

6 large egg whites, about 1 cup

¹/₂ teaspoon cream of tartar

Filling:

1¹/₂ cups heavy cream

1 teaspoon pure vanilla extract

3 tablespoons confectioners' sugar,
plus more for dusting

³/₄ cup mashed ripe banana
(about 1¹/₂ bananas)

Fresh raspberries, optional

Preheat the oven to 325°F.

Sift together the flour, sugar, baking powder, and salt in a bowl. In a large bowl with an electric mixer, beat together the oil, egg yolks, banana, lemon juice, and vanilla until well blended. Gradually add the dry ingredients, mixing on low until just incorporated. In another bowl, beat the egg whites and cream of tartar until stiff peaks form. Pour a little of the batter into the whites and fold in with a rubber spatula, then add the remainder and fold in gently (but do not beat). Pour the batter into an ungreased 10-inch tube pan with a removable bottom.

Bake for 50 to 60 minutes, or until the top of the cake springs back when lightly touched with your finger. To cool, turn the cake over and place the tube over the neck of an empty wine bottle (have no fear, the cake will not fall onto your countertop). Let the cake hang on the bottle until the pan is no longer warm (even overnight is fine).

When cool, turn the cake right side up and run a long, thin knife along the side of the pan all the way around. Lift the cake out and run the knife the same way around the bottom and around the center next to the tube. Invert onto a platter and remove the tube, then turn right side up. You can make the cake to this point even the day before. Wait until just an hour or so prior to serving before slicing and filling.

To make the filling: In a medium bowl, whip the cream with the vanilla and confectioners' sugar, until stiff peaks form. Fold in the banana.

To assemble: Use a serrated knife to slice the cake into 3 even layers. Spoon about a 1-inch thickness of the filling onto the bottom layer and repeat with the remaining layer, topping the cake with the final layer. Dust with confectioners' sugar. Spoon a pool of the dessert sauce on the plate and lay a slice horizontally on top of the sauce. Scatter a few fresh raspberries on top, if desired.

Banana-Raspberry Dessert Sauce

This is a deliciously tangy, all-purpose dessert sauce for mild-tasting cakes such as the Indonesian Coconut-Banana Cake (page 129). You can also serve it for breakfast along with butter and maple syrup over Banana Oat Waffles (page 27), or Sour Cream–Banana Pancakes (page 25).

Makes about 2 cups

2 ripe bananas, cut into chunks

1 (12-ounce) package frozen raspberries in syrup, thawed

2 teaspoons superfine sugar

1 tablespoon fresh lemon juice

Place ingredients in a food processor or blender and process until smooth. Strain the sauce through a fine-mesh sieve, pushing the pulp through with a rubber spatula and scraping from the bottom.

Banana Upside-Down Cake

Baking this in an iron skillet creates a sticky, caramel crust on top of the cake. Macadamia nuts and coconut make it special. For optimum flavor, serve the cake warm and reheat any leftovers. Although the recipe calls for finger bananas, you can also use 3 to 4 medium bananas.

Makes 6 to 8 servings

8 tablespoons unsalted butter, softened

$^1/_2$ cup packed dark brown sugar

$^1/_3$ cup sweetened, shredded coconut

$^1/_3$ cup coarsely chopped
   macadamia nuts

6 to 8 finger bananas, sliced
   lengthwise into 3 pieces

$1^1/_3$ cups all-purpose flour

2 teaspoons baking powder

$^1/_2$ teaspoon salt

$^2/_3$ cup granulated sugar

2 teaspoons finely grated lemon
   or orange zest

1 teaspoon pure vanilla extract

1 large egg

$^2/_3$ cup milk

Vanilla ice cream or whipped cream,
   optional

Preheat the oven to 350°F. Place 2 tablespoons of the butter in a 10-inch skillet, cake pan, or pie plate. Heat in the oven 10 minutes until the butter melts. Sprinkle the brown sugar, coconut, and nuts over the butter. Arrange the bananas over the bottom and sides of the pan; set aside while preparing the batter.

Stir together the flour, baking powder, and salt. In a large bowl, beat the remaining 6 tablespoons of butter, the granulated sugar, zest, vanilla, and egg with an electric mixer until pale yellow and thick. With the mixer on its lowest setting, add the flour mixture alternately with the milk, scraping down and beating about 1 minute until well blended. Scrape the batter over the bananas and spread to the edges to cover them. Bake 40 minutes, or until the top of the cake is golden and firm to the touch. Cool in the pan 10 minutes. To unmold the cake, place a large plate or platter over the skillet and quickly flip the skillet. (If any banana slices stick, gently pry them from the bottom and reposition them on top of the cake.) Serve the cake warm with vanilla ice cream or whipped cream, if desired.

Hawaiian Banana Cake

Rum, coconut, lime, and macadamia nuts lend an island touch to this delicately flavored, ultramoist banana cake. To make it extra special, place a few spoonfuls of warm Bittersweet Fudge Sauce (page 144) on the dessert plate before topping with a square of the warm cake—it's an exotic and marvelous flavor combination.

Makes one 8-inch-square cake with nine 2$^{1}/_{2}$-inch squares

2$^{1}/_{4}$ cups all-purpose flour

1 teaspoon baking powder

1 teaspoon baking soda

$^{1}/_{2}$ teaspoon freshly grated nutmeg

$^{1}/_{2}$ teaspoon ground cinnamon

$^{1}/_{2}$ teaspoon salt

$^{1}/_{2}$ cup (1 stick) plus 2 tablespoons unsalted butter, softened

$^{1}/_{2}$ cup packed light brown sugar

2 large eggs

$^{1}/_{4}$ cup buttermilk

1$^{1}/_{2}$ teaspoons finely grated lime zest (from 1 lime)

1 tablespoon fresh lime juice

3 tablespoons dark rum

1$^{1}/_{2}$ cups mashed ripe banana (about 4 spotted bananas)

$^{1}/_{2}$ cup sweetened, shredded coconut

$^{1}/_{3}$ cup chopped macadamia nuts

$^{3}/_{4}$ cup confectioners' sugar

Preheat the oven to 350°F. Grease and flour an 8-inch-square cake pan.

Stir together the flour, baking powder, baking soda, nutmeg, cinnamon, and salt and set aside. Cream together ½ cup of the butter and the brown sugar in a large bowl with an electric mixer until light and fluffy. Add the eggs, one at a time, beating well after each addition.

Combine the buttermilk, lime zest and juice, 1 tablespoon of the rum, and the banana and add to the butter-egg mixture (it will appear curdled, but don't worry). With the mixer running on its lowest setting, gradually add the flour mixture until just incorporated. Fold in the coconut and nuts with a rubber spatula. Scrape the batter into the prepared pan. Bake 40 to 45 minutes, or until a wooden skewer inserted in the center comes out clean. Place the pan on a rack to cool until warm to the touch.

Stir together the confectioners' sugar, the remaining 2 tablespoons of butter, and 2 tablespoons of rum in a small saucepan over low heat, until the butter melts and the glaze is smooth. Drizzle over the warm cake. Serve the cake warm or at room temperature.

Indonesian Coconut-Banana Cake

This recipe is based on a flourless cake in Sri Owen's remarkable Indonesian Regional Cooking. The original calls for pisang kepok, a special cooking banana native to Indonesia, but ripe plantains can be substituted. This light and delicately flavored little cake is nice served warm with honey and sweetened berries or with Banana-Raspberry Dessert Sauce (page 126). Make sure you scrape the thick coconut cream from the top and bottom of the can before adding it to the batter.

Makes one 8-inch cake, serving 6 to 8

2 ripe plantains, or 4 firm-ripe bananas

5 large eggs

³/₄ cup sugar

2 cups canned, unsweetened coconut milk, stir well

1 teaspoon pure vanilla extract

Preheat the oven to 350°F. Line an 8-inch-square baking pan with wax paper and butter the bottom and sides.

Peel and slice the plantains lengthwise, and using a serrated grapefruit spoon or the small end of a melon baller, scrape out the black seeds in the center and discard. Place the plantains in a food processor and purée (or process through a food mill).

Transfer the purée to a large bowl; using an electric mixer on medium speed, begin beating the purée. Add the eggs one at a time, beating well after each addition. Beat for 5 minutes. Add the sugar slowly and continue beating until the batter becomes thick and smooth, almost like a meringue. Pour in the coconut milk and vanilla and mix until well blended (it will lose some of its volume, but don't worry).

Scrape the batter into the prepared pan and smooth to the edges. Bake 35 to 40 minutes, or until the cake is lightly browned and the edges pull away from the sides of the pan. Leave in the pan until cool enough to serve.

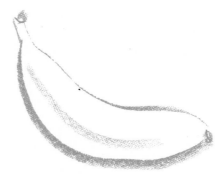

Roasted Plantain Cake with Toasted Coconut Topping

You'll want superripe plantains to make this cake. What's superripe? The plantain skins should be entirely black, soft, with fruit flies gathering on them—in other words, fruit you would normally toss. But fruit flies indicate that the plantain starch has largely turned to sugar and is at its peak flavor for use in baked goods. This recipe is from Carole Kotkin, a cooking-school teacher and coauthor of the Latin-flavored MMMMiami cookbook (Henry Holt, 1998). Roasting intensifies the sweetness of ripe plantains. If you can't find black-skinned plantains at the market, buy the soft, yellow ones, enclose them in a brown paper bag, and set them aside for a few days. Firm-ripe bananas can be used in place of the plantains. Carole suggests serving the cake with vanilla or coconut ice cream.

Makes one 9 x 13 x 2-inch cake

3 superripe, black-skinned plantains
   or 5 firm-ripe bananas
2$^{1}/_4$ cups sifted cake flour
1 tablespoon baking powder
$^{1}/_2$ teaspoon baking soda
$^{1}/_2$ teaspoon salt
$^{1}/_2$ cup (1 stick) unsalted butter, softened
1$^{1}/_4$ cups granulated sugar
2 large eggs
2 tablespoons banana liqueur or dark rum
1 teaspoon pure vanilla extract
1 cup chopped walnuts, optional

For the topping:

2$^{1}/_2$ tablespoons cold unsalted butter, cut into small pieces
$^{1}/_4$ cup packed brown sugar
1 tablespoon all-purpose flour
1 cup sweetened, shredded coconut
$^{1}/_2$ cup chopped walnuts, optional

Up to the day before making the cake, roast the plantains: Preheat the oven to 350°F. Line a baking dish with foil and place plantains, skins on, in the dish. Prick the skins with a sharp knife a few times to allow the steam to escape. Bake about 35 minutes, or until soft and puffy looking (alternately, prick the skins and place in a microwave on high power for 5 minutes, turning occasionally to cook evenly). Set aside to cool, or refrigerate until you're ready to make the cake.

Preheat the oven to 350°F. Butter and flour a 9 x 13 x 2-inch cake pan. Remove the roasted plantains from their skins and purée in a food processor until smooth; you should have about 1$^1/_2$ to 2 cups purée.

Sift the flour, baking powder, baking soda, and salt together in a bowl and set aside. Beat the butter and sugar in a large bowl with an electric mixer until light and fluffy. Add the plantain purée and beat until well blended. Beat in the eggs, one at a time, beating well after each addition. Beat in the liqueur and vanilla. With the mixer on its lowest setting, gradually add the flour mixture, beating until just incorporated. Fold in the walnuts, if using, with a rubber spatula. Scrape the batter into the prepared pan and bake 25 minutes.

Meanwhile prepare the topping: combine the butter, brown sugar, flour, coconut, and walnuts, if using, in a bowl and mix until crumbly. Remove the partially baked cake from the oven and scatter the topping across the top evenly. Bake 15 to 20 minutes longer, or until the topping is golden brown and a wooden skewer inserted in the center of the cake comes out clean. (If necessary, brown the cake beneath the broiler 1 to 2 minutes to brown the topping.) Cool the cake in the pan on a rack before slicing.

Ultimate Banana Cake with Brown Sugar Frosting

I adore this cake for its simplicity. It has an incredibly tender texture and tastes purely of butter, brown sugar, and bananas. The recipe was given to me by my friend Cindy Workman, who is frequently asked for it. Cindy usually gives the cake a light dusting of confectioners' sugar, but I also like it with an old-fashioned, brown sugar frosting that my mother used on the numerous cakes of my childhood.

Makes one 9 x 13 x 2-inch cake, or two 8-inch layers

2³/4 cups cake flour

1¹/2 teaspoons baking soda

1/2 teaspoon salt

1 cup buttermilk, at room temperature

1¹/2 teaspoons pure vanilla extract

3/4 cup mashed very ripe banana (about 2 bananas)

1/2 cup plus 2 tablespoons unsalted butter, softened

1/4 cup vegetable oil

3/4 cup packed dark brown sugar

1/2 cup granulated sugar

4 large eggs, room temperature

Brown Sugar Frosting (recipe follows)

Preheat the oven to 350°F. Butter a 9 x 13 x 2-inch baking pan. Sift together the flour, baking soda, and salt and set aside. Mix together the buttermilk, vanilla, and bananas in a separate bowl and set aside.

Cream the butter, oil, brown sugar, and granulated sugar in a large bowl with an electric mixer until light and fluffy, about 4 minutes. Add the eggs, one at a time, scraping and beating well after each addition. With the mixer on its lowest setting, add the dry ingredients alternately with the buttermilk mixture in three parts, scraping down occasionally and beating until the ingredients are just combined.

Pour the batter into the prepared pan and bake, 40 to 45 minutes, until the top is very golden and a wooden skewer inserted near the center of the cake comes out clean. Place the pan on a rack to cool completely.

Brown Sugar Frosting

This makes enough to frost a 9 x 13 x 2-inch cake or two 8-inch layers. If desired, add ¹/₂ cup chopped nuts and ¹/₂ cup sweetened, shredded coconut.

1 cup packed dark brown sugar
¹/₂ cup (1 stick) unsalted butter, softened
¹/₃ cup heavy cream

1 teaspoon pure vanilla extract
Pinch of salt
3 cups confectioners' sugar

Place the brown sugar, butter, and cream in a medium saucepan and bring to a boil. Cook 2 minutes, stirring, until the sugar is dissolved and the frosting bubbles to the top. Remove from the heat and stir in the vanilla and salt. With an electric mixer on medium speed, add 1 cup of the confectioners' sugar and beat to incorporate. Gradually add the remaining sugar, beating until the frosting is smooth and creamy. Immediately spread the frosting over the cake while it is still warm. If the frosting starts to dry or becomes crusty, return it to low heat and stir just until it becomes creamy again.

Variation

Make the cake but instead of adding frosting, slice and serve it with Rosemary Syrup (page 175) and a dollop of Greek-style, whole-milk yogurt.

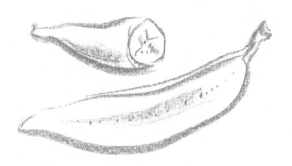

Banana Cake

Grams . . . marketed for food once or, if lucky, twice a month. She bought "precious" green bananas whenever they were available. Around 1890, Grams stored and ripened fruits in the unlighted root cellar with one door to the outside. Rubye [sic] and Mom thought they were so clever sneaking a banana or a bunch of grapes, but Grams knew all along. As you can guess, after two or three weeks, a few bananas were not in prime condition for eating as is. "Waste not, want not," in mind, Grams whisked those blemished bananas in a spicy batter, then baked and converted them into a tasty cake.

—Janeen Aletta Sarlin, *Food from an American Farm*

Chocolate-Banana Pudding Cakes

Bananas provide a creamy finish to this ultrarich, brownie-like cake that makes its own chocolate sauce as it cooks. Baking the cakes in individual coffee cups makes an elegant presentation for a dinner party. Though it's much less attractive, you can also bake this in an 8-inch square pan and spoon it into bowls. Ice cream is definitely required.

Makes 6 individual servings

4 tablespoons unsalted butter

1 cup granulated sugar

2 large eggs

1 ripe banana, mashed

1 teaspoon pure vanilla extract

1 cup all-purpose flour

1 cup unsweetened cocoa powder

$^1/_4$ teaspoon ground cinnamon

1 teaspoon baking powder

$^1/_2$ teaspoon salt

$^1/_2$ cup packed dark brown sugar

$^3/_4$ cup boiling water

Confectioners' sugar for dusting

Vanilla or coffee ice cream

Preheat the oven to 350°F. Butter six 8-ounce ironstone coffee cups (not fine china), ramekins, or custard cups. (If using coffee cups, you will also need the saucers.)

In a 2-quart saucepan, heat the butter until melted; cool slightly. Beat in the granulated sugar, eggs, banana, and vanilla. Stir together the flour, $^3/_4$ cup of the cocoa powder, cinnamon, baking powder, and salt in a separate bowl. Beat the flour mixture into the banana mixture with a wire whisk until there are no visible lumps. Divide the batter evenly among the cups. Place the cups in their saucers on a large baking sheet.

In a small bowl, whisk together the brown sugar, the remaining $^1/_4$ cup of cocoa powder, and the boiling water. Pour over the cake batter, dividing evenly among the cups. Bake 25 to 30 minutes, until the cakes are puffed and firm at the edges (they should still be soft at the center). Cool 15 minutes and dust lightly with confectioners' sugar. Serve warm with vanilla or coffee ice cream.

Coconut-Banana Cupcakes with Cream Cheese Frosting

These light and pretty cakes are impossible to resist.

Makes 16 to 18 cupcakes

1³/4 cups all-purpose flour
1/2 teaspoon baking powder
1/2 teaspoon baking soda
1/4 teaspoon salt
1/2 cup mashed ripe banana
(about 1¹/4 bananas)
1/4 cup buttermilk
1/2 teaspoon pure vanilla extract
1 teaspoon pure almond extract

1/2 cup (1 stick) unsalted butter, softened
1 cup sugar
3 large eggs
1 (7-ounce) package sweetened, shredded coconut, poured into a bowl and fluffed with a fork to separate flakes
Cream Cheese Frosting (recipe follows)

Preheat the oven to 325°F. Line ¹/2-cup muffin tins with paper baking cups.

Stir together the flour, baking powder, baking soda, and salt and set aside. Mix the banana, buttermilk, vanilla, and almond extract together and set aside.

Beat the butter and sugar in a large mixing bowl with an electric mixer until very light and fluffy, about 4 minutes. With the mixer running on its lowest setting, add the eggs, one at a time, beating well after each addition.

Add the dry ingredients to the batter in halves, alternating with the buttermilk mixture, until just combined. Using a rubber spatula, fold in 1¹/3 cups of the fluffed coconut until incorporated.

Spoon the batter into the muffin cups, filling each to ¹/4-inch below the top. Bake for 25 minutes, or until a toothpick inserted in the center comes out clean. Cool cupcakes in the pan for 10 minutes, then transfer them to a wire rack to cool completely. Frost and top with the remaining coconut.

Cream Cheese Frosting

Makes about 2¹/₂ cups,
enough for 18 cupcakes

1 (8-ounce) package cream cheese,
  softened
6 tablespoons unsalted butter, softened

¹/₂ teaspoon pure vanilla extract
¹/₂ teaspoon pure almond extract
3 cups confectioners' sugar, sifted

Beat together the cream cheese, butter, vanilla, and the almond extract in a medium bowl with an electric mixer. Gradually add the sugar and beat until smooth and creamy.

Pies, Tarts, and Puddings

Knock, knock

Who's there?

Banana

Banana who?

Knock, knock

Who's there?

Banana

Banana who?

Knock, knock

Who's there?

Orange

Orange who?

Orange you glad I didn't say banana?

—Famous knock, knock joke

Classic Banana Cream Pie

This banana cream pie has just the right combination of everything you'd ever want in a pie: an ultra-flaky crust, a lusciously sweet and creamy filling, and just enough bananas to make it fabulous. The variations that follow for chocolate- and coconut-banana cream pies are equally wonderful.

Makes 6 servings

Flaky Pie Crust (recipe follows)

Filling:

1/4 cup cornstarch

Pinch of salt

1/2 cup sugar

4 large egg yolks

2 3/4 cups whole milk

2 tablespoons unsalted butter

1 1/2 teaspoons pure vanilla extract

2 ripe bananas

Topping:

1 cup heavy cream

2 tablespoons sugar

1 teaspoon pure vanilla extract

Whisk together the cornstarch, salt, and sugar in a medium saucepan until there are no visible lumps. Beat the egg yolks into the milk in a medium bowl. Slowly whisk the egg-milk mixture in a stream into the cornstarch mixture over medium heat. Whisk all along the bottom and sides of the pan continuously until the mixture comes to a boil. Reduce heat to low and stir until the custard thickens, about 3 to 5 minutes. (The filling will seem a bit thin, but it will become firm as it cools.) Remove the pan from the heat and stir in the butter and vanilla. Place a circle of wax paper over the top of the filling, pressing down so that no air is trapped; cool 20 minutes. Slice the bananas 1/4-inch thick. Using a rubber spatula, fold the bananas into the filling and then pour it into the shell.

Use an electric hand mixer to whip the cream, sugar, and vanilla until it holds firm peaks. Spread the topping over the filling, making sure it touches the edges of the pastry all around. You can refrigerate the pie several hours before serving time, but allow it to warm up to room temperature before serving.

Flaky Pie Crust

*Makes enough for one
9- or 10-inch pie crust*

1½ cups all-purpose flour

1 tablespoon sugar

¼ teaspoon salt

6 tablespoons cold unsalted butter,
    cut into small pieces

2 tablespoons cold Crisco shortening

1 large egg yolk, beaten

2 to 3 tablespoons ice water

Food processor method: Place all ingredients except the yolk and water into a food processor and pulse at 1-second intervals until the mixture resembles coarse cornmeal. Add the egg yolk and sprinkle 2 tablespoons of the water over the flour-butter mixture and pulse until the dough begins to clump together (add a little more water if necessary).

Hand method: Stir together the flour, sugar, and salt in a large bowl. Add the butter and shortening, and using your fingertips or a pastry blender, blend the fats into the flour until the mixture looks like coarse crumbs. Add the egg yolk and sprinkle the water over the flour-butter mixture; stir with a fork to incorporate the water (it will still seem rather clumpy but should hold together).

Turn the dough out onto a large piece of plastic wrap. Using your hands, gather the dough together to form a ball. Press it with your palms to form a 1-inch-thick disk. Wrap it up and refrigerate for at least 30 minutes.

On a lightly floured surface with a floured rolling pin, roll the dough into a 15-inch circle. Place in a 9-inch (preferably glass) pie plate. Trim away all but 1 inch of the overhanging dough. Turn it under the rim and flute the edges. Pierce the crust all over with the tines of a fork at $\frac{1}{2}$-inch intervals. Chill the pie crust 30 minutes, until firm.

To prebake the crust: Preheat the oven to 350°F and position the rack in the middle. Line the pie crust with a circle of waxed paper (bigger than the pie plate so it is easy to remove pie weights later) and fill it with pie weights or dried beans. Bake 20 minutes and remove the wax paper and pie weights. Return to the oven and bake until the crust is a deep golden brown, about 5 to 10 minutes (keep checking every few minutes). Cool the crust on a rack and proceed with the filling recipe, above.

Variations

Chocolate-banana cream pie: Reduce the sugar in the filling to $\frac{1}{3}$ cup and add 4 ounces of finely chopped semisweet chocolate in with the butter and vanilla, whisking thoroughly until it has melted. Cool and fold in the banana slices as directed. Sprinkle chocolate shavings on top of the whipped cream.

Coconut-banana cream pie: After the filling has cooled, fold in $\frac{1}{2}$ cup sweetened, shredded coconut. Sprinkle $\frac{1}{4}$ cup toasted coconut on top of the whipped cream.

Frozen Caramel-Banana Cream Pie

In this luscious pie, the filling is caramelized, rather than the bananas. Cooking the condensed milk takes time, but because it's done in the oven, there's no stirring required. You can put the pie together and pop it in the freezer the morning before a dinner party. It has a creamy, frozen mousselike texture with the buttery crunch of candied walnuts on top.

Makes 6 to 8 servings

Graham Cracker–Nut Crust
  (recipe follows)
1 (14-ounce) can sweetened,
  condensed milk
1 tablespoon butter

1 tablespoon sugar
$^1/_3$ cup chopped walnuts
3 to 4 bananas
2 cups heavy whipping cream

Preheat the oven to 400°F. Pour the milk into an 8-inch pie plate (preferably metal). Cover with foil. Place the pie plate in a larger pan and pour about 1-inch of boiling water into it. Bake 1 hour and 20 minutes, or until the milk is thick and has a deep caramel color. Leave it covered and set aside to cool to room temperature (or place in the refrigerator to speed up the process).

Melt the butter and sugar in a skillet over medium heat. Add the walnuts and cook, stirring, until coated and lightly golden brown. Set aside to cool.

Slice 1 to 2 bananas crosswise $^1/_8$-inch thick. Line the bottom of the graham cracker crust with banana slices.

Using an electric mixer, whip the cream until it holds stiff peaks. Add a large dollop of the whipped cream to the caramelized milk to lighten it. Then fold (but don't beat) with a rubber spatula the caramelized milk into the whipped cream until blended. Spoon half of the walnut filling on top of the bananas in the crust. Place another layer of sliced bananas over the filling. Top with the remaining filling. Place in the freezer at least 2 hours, until solid. Remove from the freezer and arrange banana slices around the rim. Scatter the walnuts on top. Slice the frozen pie and place on plates. Let pie slices sit out at room temperature for 15 minutes before serving.

Graham Cracker–Nut Crust

Makes enough for one
9-inch pie

1 cup graham cracker crumbs
   (10 cracker rectangles)
1/2 cup finely chopped walnuts

1/3 cup butter, softened to room
   temperature
2 tablespoons sugar

Preheat the oven to 350°F. Blend the crumbs, walnuts, butter, and sugar in a bowl. Firmly press the mixture on the bottom and sides of a buttered, 9-inch glass pie dish. Bake 8 to 10 minutes, until the crust is lightly toasted. Cool to room temperature before filling.

Bittersweet Fudge Sauce

This is the ideal hot fudge sauce that stays creamy as you pour it warm over ice cream.

Makes 2¹/₂ cups, enough for Ice Cream Pie (recipe follows) and leftovers

6 ounces fine-quality bittersweet chocolate

4 tablespoons unsalted butter

¹/₂ cup unsweetened cocoa powder

1¹/₂ cups heavy cream

5 tablespoons light corn syrup

¹/₄ cup sugar

Pinch of salt

1 tablespoon dark rum

2 teaspoons pure vanilla extract

Melt the chocolate and butter in the top of a double boiler over barely simmering water or in a glass bowl placed in the microwave for 1 minute. Stir in the cocoa with a whisk. Put the cream, corn syrup, sugar, and salt in a medium saucepan and bring to a boil. Remove from the heat and stir in the rum, vanilla, and the melted chocolate mixture. Cool the sauce until almost room temperature. You can store any leftover fudge sauce in a jar in the refrigerator for up to 1 month.

Ice Cream Pie with Bittersweet Fudge Sauce

This is one of those over-the-top, rich chocolate desserts that we all need to indulge in once in a while, just to feel wicked. It's also very easy to put together and pop in the freezer. You can use a purchased chocolate sauce to speed things up, but I've yet to try one that has the deep, bittersweet chocolate taste of this fudge sauce.

Makes 6 servings

1^1/$_2$ cups Bittersweet Fudge Sauce (preceding recipe)

1 Oreo-brand chocolate cookie crust

2^1/$_2$ ripe red bananas (or 1^1/$_2$ large yellow bananas), thinly sliced

2^3/$_4$ cups (a little less than 1^1/$_2$ pints) Häagen-Dazs Dulce de Leche (caramel) ice cream (or vanilla), slightly softened

Whipped cream for garnish

Make Fudge Sauce first. Spoon a small amount of the fudge sauce in the bottom of the crust and line it with banana slices. Using a rubber spatula, scoop up about 1½ cups of the ice cream (being careful not to stir up the caramel sauce), and spoon it over the bananas in the crust, gently smoothing to the edges. Add another layer of banana slices and top with the remaining ice cream.

Drizzle the top of the pie with about ½ cup of the fudge sauce. Freeze the pie at least 5 hours, or overnight, until firm.

Allow the pie to sit at room temperature 15 minutes before slicing with a knife dipped in warm water. Heat the remaining fudge sauce and pool a small amount onto each dessert plate before topping with a slice of pie. Drizzle with more sauce and add a dollop of whipped cream.

Singing the Chiquita Song

*I*f you happened to be born in a certain era, you can no doubt hum a few bars of the Chiquita jingle, one of the most famous advertising jingles ever written. It hit the airwaves when Miss Chiquita was introduced, and its purpose was to instruct as well as entertain. At its peak, the jingle was played 376 times a day on radio stations. The song was created by a BBDO advertising agency team headed by Robert Foreman. He and his staff wrote the song on an old piano, shaking a box of paper clips to mimic the sounds of maracas. Garth Montgomery wrote the lyrics and Ken MacKenzie provided the music. The first singer to record the song was Patti Clayton, the first in a long line of Miss Chiquitas.

"I'm Chiquita Banana and I've come to say—

bananas have to ripen in a certain way—

When they're fleck'd with brown and have a golden hue—

Bananas taste the best and are best for you—

You can put them in a salad—

You can put them in a pie-aye—

Any way you want to eat them—

It's impossible to beat them—

But, bananas like the climate of the very, very tropical equator—

So you should never put bananas in the refrigerator."

—Music copyrighted 1945 by Shawnee Press, Inc.

Chocolate-Nut Banana Tarts

These are wonderfully simple tarts that taste as if you bought them in a fancy bakery, even though they are made with frozen puff pastry from the supermarket. Splurge on a good bar of French or Swiss chocolate—it makes all the difference.

Makes 4 servings

1 sheet frozen puff pastry, thawed but still cold

2 to 3 large firm-ripe bananas

3 ounces fine-quality bittersweet or semisweet chocolate, finely chopped

$^1/2$ cup chopped pecans or walnuts, lightly toasted

4 tablespoons sugar

2 tablespoons cold unsalted butter, cut into small pieces

Vanilla ice cream, optional

Unfold the pastry sheet on a lightly floured surface and slice it in half. Roll each half out into a 10 x 5-inch rectangle. Cut each rectangle in half to form four 5-inch squares.

Arrange the squares on 2 large baking sheets, about 2 inches apart. Sprinkle the squares evenly with the chocolate, leaving a $^1/2$-inch border along the edges. Slice the bananas on the diagonal into $^1/4$-inch-thick slices. Beginning from the outside edges and working your way to the center, arrange the banana slices—slightly overlapping them—into a square pattern so that the top of the tart is covered. Sprinkle the tops evenly with the chopped pecans, sugar, and butter pieces. Chill in the refrigerator 15 minutes. Preheat the oven to 425°F.

Bake the tarts in the middle of the oven, in batches if necessary, 10 to 15 minutes, or until the pastry is golden brown on the bottom and cooked through. Serve the tarts at room temperature or warm with vanilla ice cream, if desired.

Union Square Cafe's Caramel-Banana Tart

According to owner Danny Meyer, this tart is far and away the most popular dessert at the famed Union Square Cafe in New York. This recipe is adapted from The Union Square Cafe Cookbook *(HarperCollins, 1994). One taste and you know it's a very special dessert—and it's not all that difficult to make at home. The bananas are sliced fresh and placed on top of the tart crust, barely warmed then drizzled all over—Jackson Pollack fashion— with hot caramel and topped with macadamia nuts.*

Makes 6 servings

Crust:

^{1}/$_2$ cup (1 stick) unsalted butter, softened

^{1}/$_4$ cup sugar

1 large egg yolk

1 teaspoon pure vanilla extract

^{1}/$_4$ teaspoon salt

1 cup all-purpose flour

Banana topping:

^{1}/$_2$ cup plus 1 tablespoon sugar

1 tablespoon light corn syrup

2 tablespoons unsalted butter, melted

4 large ripe bananas, thinly sliced on the diagonal

1 cup (about 5 ounces) chopped macadamia nuts, lightly toasted

Vanilla ice cream, optional

To make the crust: Beat the butter and the sugar in a large bowl with an electric mixer. Beat in the egg yolk, vanilla, and salt and blend well. Add the flour and beat until moist clumps begin to form. Press the dough with your hands onto the bottom of a 9-inch tart pan with a removable bottom. Pierce with a fork in a few places, about 2 inches apart. Refrigerate for 1 hour. Preheat the oven to 450°F. Bake the crust until golden, about 15 minutes. Set aside to cool.

To make the topping: Place a large baking pan filled halfway with cold water and a few ice cubes next to the stove. Combine ½ cup of the sugar, the corn syrup, and 1 tablespoon of the melted butter in a small saucepan over medium heat. Heat the mixture until the sugar dissolves and it comes to a boil. Boil the mixture, without stirring but swirling the pan occasionally so that it browns evenly, until it turns a medium amber color, about 7 minutes. Place the pan in the ice water to prevent further cooking and to cool it to lukewarm.

Preheat the oven to 375°F. Arrange the banana slices, overlapping them slightly, in a concentric circle beginning at the crust edge and working your way in so that the crust is completely covered. Brush the remaining tablespoon of butter over the bananas and sprinkle with the remaining tablespoon of sugar. Bake until the tart is just warmed through, about 3 to 5 minutes.

Rewarm the caramel topping over low heat, stirring occasionally. Remove the tart from the oven. Dip a spoon into the caramel and drizzle it back and forth in squiggly lines over the bananas. Remove the pan bottom and place the tart on a platter or large plate. Scatter the nuts over the top, slice and serve warm with vanilla ice cream, if desired.

Warm Banana-Custard Tart

Another irresistible banana tart with an eggy, rum-flavored custard that's a perfect base for bananas.

Makes 8 servings

Crust:

¹/2 cup (1 stick) unsalted butter, softened

1¹/2 cups all-purpose flour

²/3 cup finely chopped cashews

1 large egg, lightly beaten

¹/2 teaspoon pure vanilla extract

Custard Filling:

2 large eggs

¹/2 cup sugar

2 tablespoons all-purpose flour

³/4 cup heavy cream

3 tablespoons dark rum

3 to 4 ripe bananas, thinly sliced

2 cups unsweetened whipped cream, optional

Combine all the crust ingredients in the bowl of a food processor (or use an electric mixer). Pulse or beat until the dough is smooth. Press the dough with your hands onto the bottom of a 9-inch tart pan with a removable bottom. Pierce with a fork in a few places, about 2 inches apart. Refrigerate for 1 hour. Preheat the oven to 400°F. Bake the crust until golden, about 15 to 20 minutes. Set aside to cool while you make the custard.

Preheat the oven to 350°F. Beat the eggs with the sugar in a large bowl using an electric mixer until light and fluffy. Add the flour and mix until smooth. Add the cream and rum and blend well. Pour the mixture into the prebaked tart shell and bake 20 minutes, or until the custard is set. Top the tart with the sliced bananas, arranging them in a circular pattern starting from the crust inward. Slice the tart and serve warm with a dollop of unsweetened whipped cream, if desired.

Banana Bread Pudding with Custard Sauce

Do you have some ripe bananas and day-old bread? Then you have the makings of a luscious, comforting dessert. Make the sauce first—even the day before is fine—and reheat it before serving.

Makes 6 to 8 servings

Custard Sauce (recipe follows)

4 cups 1-inch cubes, day-old country white bread

4 tablespoons butter, melted

2 cups whole milk

3/4 cup heavy cream

1/3 cup granulated sugar

2 teaspoons pure vanilla extract

1/4 teaspoon freshly grated nutmeg

3 large eggs

3 tablespoons light brown sugar

2 ripe bananas, thinly sliced

Toss the bread cubes with 2 tablespoons of the melted butter. In a large bowl, whisk together the milk, cream, granulated sugar, vanilla, nutmeg, and eggs until well blended. Add the bread cubes to the bowl and stir to coat; let stand 15 minutes.

Preheat the oven to 325°F and butter an 8-inch-square baking dish or a shallow 2-quart casserole. Heat the remaining 2 tablespoons butter and the brown sugar in a large nonstick skillet over medium heat until the mixture begins to simmer and the sugar dissolves. Add the bananas and cook about 1 minute, stirring to coat the bananas with the sugar mixture. Stir the cooked bananas into the soaked bread cubes. Transfer to the baking dish. Bake 45 minutes, or until a knife inserted in the center comes out clean. Cool in the pan on a wire rack about 30 minutes. Cut into 6 or 8 even slices. Spoon a pool of sauce onto each dessert plate and place a slice of the pudding on top. Pour a little more sauce over the top.

Custard Sauce

2¹/₂ cups low- or reduced-fat milk

1 vanilla bean, split, or 2 teaspoons pure vanilla extract, optional

1 strip orange peel

2 large eggs

¹/₃ cup sugar

Rinse a saucepan with cold water and shake dry (this helps prevent sticking). Add the milk, the vanilla bean (but not the extract, if using), if using, and the orange peel and bring the mixture almost to a boil. Remove from the heat, cover, and set aside to steep for 30 minutes.

Return the milk to a simmer. Meanwhile whisk the eggs and sugar in a bowl until smooth but not fluffy. Gradually whisk in about half of the hot milk to warm the eggs, then pour all of the egg mixture into the simmering milk. Cook the custard over low heat, stirring constantly, until the mixture thickens enough to coat the back of a spoon, about 7 to 8 minutes (do not let it boil).

Strain the custard into a clean bowl. Scrape the seeds from the vanilla bean into the custard or stir in the vanilla extract, if using. Cool in the refrigerator, stirring once or twice. Once chilled, cover the bowl with plastic wrap until ready to use.

Banana Clafouti

Clafouti is a traditional French pudding, usually made with fresh black cherries. Made with bananas, it's a comforting dessert perfect for a cool winter evening.

Makes 6 servings

5 tablespoons granulated sugar

5 to 6 ripe finger or baby bananas
  (or 3 medium bananas)

1^1/$_2$ cups whole milk

3 large eggs

^{1}/$_2$ cup all-purpose flour

1 tablespoon freshly grated orange zest

1 teaspoon pure vanilla extract

Pinch of salt

Confectioners' sugar for dusting

Preheat the oven to 350°F. Butter a 10-inch, deep-dish pie plate or a 7 x 10-inch, shallow baking dish. Sprinkle the bottom with 2 tablespoons of the sugar. Slice each banana into 3 lengthwise strips and arrange, slightly overlapping, on the bottom of the dish.

Place the remaining 3 tablespoons of sugar, the milk, eggs, flour, orange zest, vanilla, and salt in a blender and purée until smooth. Pour over the bananas. Bake 40 to 50 minutes, or until the pudding is puffed and golden. Cool on a rack 15 minutes. Sift a little confectioners' sugar over the top and serve warm.

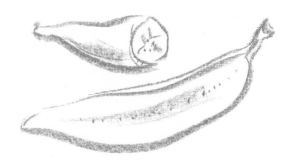

Warm Vanilla Wafer and Banana Pudding

England may have its trifle, but Americans have banana and vanilla-wafer pudding to call their own. Taking a bite of this dessert is like plunging headlong back to your childhood. Served warm, the rich, vanilla pudding tastes like scrumptious crème anglaise. You'll want to let the pudding set in a warm place while you have dinner so the wafers soften before you make the meringue. If you prefer your pudding cold, refrigerate it for several hours and top it with whipped cream instead.

Makes 8 to 10 servings

²/₃ cup sugar

¹/₃ cup cornstarch

Pinch of salt

2 cups half-and-half

2 cups whole milk

4 large eggs, separated

2 teaspoons pure vanilla extract

1 cup sour cream

1 (12-ounce) package vanilla wafers

6 to 8 ripe bananas

Meringue:

7 egg whites

Pinch of cream of tartar

6 tablespoons sugar

Mix the sugar, cornstarch, and salt together in a medium saucepan. Stir together the half-and-half, milk, and egg yolks. Gradually whisk the wet ingredients into the dry. Cook over medium heat, whisking constantly, until the pudding mixture becomes smooth and thickened. Fold in the vanilla and sour cream.

In a 4-quart, ovenproof glass (such as Pyrex) or ceramic dish, line the bottom with about a third of the vanilla wafers in a single layer. Slice about 2 of the bananas very thinly and place a single layer of bananas over the wafers. Pour a third of the pudding on top of the bananas. Repeat until all of the ingredients are used, ending with a layer of the pudding. (Allow the pudding to sit at least 20 minutes, or until after dinner, in a warm place.)

Preheat the oven to 400°F. Beat the egg whites in a large bowl with an electric mixer until medium peaks form. Add the cream of tartar and continue to beat. As the peaks get stiffer, begin adding the sugar, a tablespoon at a time. Beat until the meringue becomes very stiff and glossy but is not dry. Spoon the meringue lightly on top of the banana pudding, sealing the edges to the bowl. Bake 6 to 8 minutes, or until the top turns a golden caramel brown. Immediately spoon the pudding with a scoop of meringue into small bowls.

Variation

Grand Marnier Banana Pudding: Prepare the pudding filling as directed above, but after stirring in the sour cream, cover the mixture with plastic wrap, pressing the plastic against the surface to seal out air; cool to room temperature.

Split 20 purchased ladyfingers in half lengthwise and place flat side up on a baking sheet. Toast in a 350°F oven 5 to 10 minutes until crisp. Place a third of the ladyfingers on the bottom of the bowl and brush ladyfingers lightly with $\frac{1}{2}$ cup melted raspberry jam. Sprinkle with $\frac{1}{4}$ cup Grand Marnier. Place a third of the ladyfingers, jam side up, on the bottom of a large serving bowl. Top with $1\frac{1}{2}$ sliced bananas. Add a third of the cooled pudding on top. Repeat with 1 more layer of ladyfingers, bananas, and pudding. For the final layer, brush ladyfingers with jam and arrange them, jam side down, on top of the pudding, like the spokes of a wheel. Cover with plastic wrap and refrigerate at least 8 hours or overnight. Just before serving, spread a layer of whipped cream over top. Garnish with sliced almonds or fresh raspberries, if desired. Makes 8 to 10 servings.

More Banana Desserts and Extras

Banananananananana

I thought I'd win the spelling bee

And get right to the top

But I started to spell banana

And didn't know when to stop.

—William Cole

Bananas Foster

New Orleans was a major seaport in the early to mid-1800s when exotic bananas were first brought to this country on ships from the tropics. There is a long history of banana desserts in this great Southern city, and perhaps the most famous of all is Bananas Foster, which originated at Brennan's restaurant. The flambéed banana finale became popular in the 1950s and was named for a popular patron, Richard Foster. It's still the restaurant's most popular dessert (they go through 35,000 pounds of bananas every year) and is offered at both breakfast and dinner. Here's a version that includes banana liqueur as well as rum.

Makes 4 servings

4 firm-ripe bananas

$^1/_3$ cup dark rum

2 tablespoons banana liqueur

4 tablespoons unsalted butter

$^1/_4$ cup packed dark brown sugar

Sour cream or crème fraîche for garnish

Vanilla ice cream, optional

Peel the bananas and cut them in half lengthwise. Pour the rum and banana liqueur into a glass measuring cup and heat in the microwave for 30 seconds, or warm them in a saucepan over low heat. Melt 2 tablespoons of the butter in a large, preferably nonstick, skillet over medium heat. Add 2 tablespoons of the brown sugar and swirl the pan until it is dissolved. Place 4 of the banana halves, cut side down, into the pan and cook about 2 minutes per side, turning very carefully with a large spatula.

Remove the pan from the heat and pour in half the rum mixture. Stand back from stove as you return the pan to the heat and shake it to allow the liquor to ignite. (If it fails, carefully light it with a match.) Allow the alcohol to burn off, and spoon the sauce over the bananas. Transfer to warm plates and repeat with the remaining bananas and ingredients. Garnish bananas with a small dollop of sour cream or crème fraîche, or vanilla ice cream, if desired.

Is That a Banana in Your Pocket or
Are You Just Glad to See Me?

*I*n her book, *No Go the Bogeyman: Scaring, Lulling, and Making Mock* (Farrar, Straus and Giroux, 1998), author Marina Warner devotes an entire chapter to the symbolism of the banana in popular culture, music, film, art, and literature. "The mere look of a banana and the sound of the word are funny," she says.

In short, its phallic shape and association with the virile organ is a single entendre that makes us giggle. The sexualizing of the fruit is apparent in Andy Warhol's famous album cover for the 1967 Velvet Underground and Nico's album featuring a banana that could be peeled to reveal a fleshy pink banana beneath (it's a hot collectible if you run across one at a yard sale). Dance sensation Josephine Baker tantalized audiences in the 1920s at the Follies Bergère with nothing but a string of vibrating bananas about her naked waist. It makes you wonder if it isn't a hidden Freudian desire that causes us to reach for the banana before any other fruit.

Banana Soufflés with Rum Cream

Makes 4 servings

2 ripe bananas, sliced

1 tablespoon fresh lemon juice

1 tablespoon banana liqueur, optional

$1/4$ cup packed dark brown sugar

Salt

4 large eggs, separated

$1/4$ teaspoon cream of tartar

2 tablespoons granulated sugar

$1/2$ cup heavy cream

1 tablespoon confectioners' sugar

1 tablespoon dark rum

Butter four 1-cup souffle dishes and lightly sprinkle the bottom and sides with granulated sugar. Preheat the oven to 375°F.

To make the soufflés: Combine the banana, lemon juice, liqueur, brown sugar, and a pinch of salt in a large bowl. Mash ingredients with a potato masher or fork until the sugar is dissolved. Add the yolks and beat in to combine.

Place the egg whites, cream of tartar, and a pinch of salt in a medium bowl and beat with an electric mixer until they form medium peaks. Gradually add the granulated sugar and continue beating until the egg whites hold stiff peaks. Stir a little of the egg whites into the banana mixture to lighten it. Gently fold in the remaining whites until thoroughly blended. Divide the soufflé mixture evenly among the prepared cups and place them on a large baking sheet. Bake about 20 minutes, or until the soufflés are puffed and lightly golden on top.

To make the rum cream: Whip the cream with the confectioners' sugar into stiff peaks. Beat in the rum. Just before serving, crack the soufflé tops with a large spoon and ladle a few spoonfuls of the whipped cream inside them.

Butterscotch Waffles with Bananas Cooked in Caramel Cream

This brown-sugar waffle recipe comes from Dorie Greenspan, author of Waffles: From Morning to Midnight *(William Morrow, 1993). Topped with bananas cooked in an ultrarich caramel sauce and vanilla ice cream, a dessert is born. There are a couple of steps involved, but it's not so laborious if you make the waffles ahead of time—either earlier in the day or even days ahead since they freeze well. Just warm them up in a 350°F oven for 10 minutes. These were made in a Belgian waffle iron, but if you don't have one, simply follow the manufacturer's directions for the amount of batter required per grid.*

Makes 4 servings

1 cup all-purpose flour

1 teaspoon baking powder

1/4 teaspoon ground cinnamon

1/4 cup packed light brown sugar

1 cup milk

1 large egg

1/2 teaspoon pure vanilla extract

3 tablespoons unsalted butter, melted

1/2 cup butterscotch chips, chopped

Caramel bananas:

4 firm-ripe bananas

1/3 cup unsalted butter

3/4 cup packed dark brown sugar

3/4 cup heavy cream

4 large scoops vanilla ice cream

To make the waffles: Lightly spray a Belgian waffle iron with vegetable oil and heat according to manufacturer's directions. Preheat your oven to 200°F.

In a large bowl, whisk together the flour, baking powder, cinnamon, and brown sugar. In another bowl, whisk together the milk, egg, and vanilla. Pour into the dry ingredients and stir until just combined. Fold in the butter and butterscotch chips. Ladle about 1/3 cup into each section of the waffle grid and use a wooden spoon to spread the batter almost to the edges. Close the lid and bake 5 to 6 minutes, or until no more steam emerges from the waffle iron. (The butterscotch chips may scorch a little but don't be alarmed.) Transfer the cooked waffles to a baking sheet placed in the oven (or set aside until ready to use and then reheat). Repeat with remaining batter, spraying waffle grids with vegetable oil in between batches. Makes 5 or 6 Belgian waffles.

To make the caramel bananas: Slice the bananas in half, then slice the halves lengthwise. In a large 12-inch skillet, heat the butter and brown sugar over medium heat until the butter melts and the sugar begins to bubble and dissolve. Whisk in the cream and stir until the mixture is well blended. Bring to a low simmer and add the banana pieces. Cook 1 to 2 minutes, until the bananas are heated through and are just beginning to soften (they should still be firm). Place a waffle in the center of a dessert plate and top with a scoop of ice cream. With a large spatula, arrange 4 banana pieces on top of the waffle around the ice cream and spoon more caramel sauce over all. Serve immediately.

G kluey Buad Chi

Bananas Stewed in Coconut Milk

When Thai women are ordained as Buddhist nuns, they dress in white robes. This charming dish is named for them. Roughly translated, it means "bananas ordained as nuns," for the bananas, too, are cooked and dressed in the creamy white coconut milk. This simple and elegant dish is a perfect way to end a spicy Thai meal. Regular Cavendish bananas become a bit too mushy cooked this way, but whole ripe finger bananas maintain their shape and firm texture.

Makes 4 servings

3 cups unsweetened, canned coconut
   milk, stir well

$^1/_3$ to $^1/_2$ cup sugar, depending on taste

Pinch of salt

12 ripe finger bananas

Combine the coconut milk, sugar, and salt in a medium saucepan and bring to a gentle simmer, stirring to dissolve the sugar. Add the bananas and bring the milk back to a gentle simmer. Cook 4 minutes, uncovered, until the bananas are just heated through. Transfer to small bowls and serve warm or chilled.

Sopaipillas

Puffed Banana Pillows

These puffy, crisp-fried pastries look like little pillows. They're a traditional treat of the Southwest, where they are believed to have originated, over 200 years ago. Not always made with bananas, they're sometimes stuffed with savory meat or bean fillings.

Makes 30

^{1}/3 cup superfine sugar

1 teaspoon ground cardamom

^{1}/4 teaspoon ground cinnamon

2^1/4 cups all-purpose flour

2 teaspoons baking powder

1 teaspoon salt

2 tablespoons vegetable shortening

1 cup mashed ripe bananas
   (about 2^1/2 bananas)

4 to 5 cups vegetable oil for frying

Stir together the sugar, cardamom, and cinnamon in a small bowl. Combine the flour, baking powder, salt, and shortening in the bowl of a food processor and pulse a few times until the mixture resembles coarse cornmeal. Add about 2 tablespoons water and the banana, and pulse until it forms a dough, adding more water, if necessary. Turn the dough out onto a lightly floured surface and knead it, sprinkling with a little more flour, until it becomes smooth and is no longer sticky. Roll the dough out until it is quite thin, about ⅛-inch thick. Use a ruler to mark off 3-inch squares. Cut out the squares (a pizza cutter works well), but leave them on the counter for now, and cover with barely damp paper towels.

Heat 2½ to 3 inches of oil to 375°F in an electric skillet, deep fryer, or a large pot with a thermometer attached. Line a large baking sheet with several thicknesses of paper towels. Using a large spatula, transfer a few of the squares at a time to the hot oil. Fry 1 to 2 minutes, turning once, until the squares become puffed and golden. Transfer to the baking sheet to drain. Dip each square into the spiced sugar and serve immediately. (Alternately, you can keep the sopaipillas warm in a 200°F oven until ready to serve.)

Melon and Banana Carpaccio with Honey-Mint Syrup

The peach-colored flesh of the red banana with cantaloupe and black-berries makes a dessert as pretty as it is delicious. You can use a mandoline or similar tool to obtain extra-thin melon slices.

Makes 4 servings

Syrup:

1 lemon

1 lime

$1/3$ cup mild-flavored honey

$1/2$ cup coarsely chopped mint, plus whole leaves for garnish

$1/2$ ripe cantaloupe or honeydew melon

2 ripe red bananas

$1/2$ cup plump blackberries, or sliced strawberries

With a vegetable peeler, remove all of the bright yellow and green peel of the lemon and lime. Juice and strain the lemon and lime. Place the peels, juices, and the honey in a small saucepan and bring to a boil, stirring to dissolve the honey. Remove from the heat and stir in the mint. Set aside to cool to room temperature. Strain and discard peels and mint.

Cut medium-size wedges from the melon and cut away the rind and tough, green flesh. Using a sharp knife or a mandoline, follow the curve of the melon to make long, thin slices. Arrange on a platter and place in the refrigerator until ready to use. Just before serving, peel the bananas and make long, thin slices approximately the same width. Arrange on top of the melon. Drizzle lightly with the honey syrup and garnish with mint leaves and blackberries.

Banana Fool with Fresh Mango

A fool is a mousselike dessert that's simple to make. It can also be used as a topping—like flavored whipped cream—with other desserts such as Spicy Banana Gingerbread (page 119). If you can't find mango, substitute any ripe, seasonal fruit such as peaches, melon, or berries.

Makes 6 servings

3 ripe bananas, sliced

2 tablespoons fresh lime juice

1/4 cup plus 1 tablespoon sugar

1 cup heavy cream

2 ripe mangoes, peeled and thinly sliced

2 tablespoons minced crystallized ginger

Place bananas in the bowl of a food processor with the lime juice and 1/4 cup of the sugar. Pulse until smooth.

In another bowl, beat the cream with the remaining tablespoon of sugar until it forms stiff peaks. Fold in the banana purée. Divide the fool between 6 stemmed glasses. Arrange mango slices around the fool and sprinkle the tops with the ginger. Serve immediately or refrigerate for 1 hour.

Icebox Cheesecake

If no-bake cheesecake makes you think of graham-cracker-crust-and-cherry-pie-filling desserts that your grandmother used to make, this pie will change your opinion of them forever. The buttery cookie crust alone is worth the effort; the banana-flavored filling is lightly sweet and smooth, and the prettily arranged fruit on top is fresh and juicy.

Makes 8 servings

Crust:

1/4 cup (1/2 stick) unsalted butter, melted

1/2 teaspoon pure almond extract

2 cups vanilla-wafer cookie crumbs

Filling:

8 ounces Philadelphia-brand cream cheese, at room temperature

1/3 cup confectioners' sugar

1/2 cup heavy cream

2 tablespoons banana liqueur, or 1 teaspoon pure vanilla extract

1/2 teaspoon pure almond extract

1 to 2 ripe bananas, sliced 1/4-inch thick

2 ripe kiwis, peeled and sliced 1/4-inch thick

1 (1/2-pint) basket fresh blackberries

1/4 cup red currant jam

To make the crust: Preheat the oven to 325°F and butter a 9-inch glass pie dish. Combine the melted butter, almond extract, and cookie crumbs, and use your hands to firmly press the crumb mixture onto the bottom and up the sides of the pie dish. Bake the crust until it is lightly toasted, about 10 minutes. Set aside to cool completely.

To make the filling: Blend the cream cheese with an electric mixer until smooth. Add the sugar, cream, banana liqueur, and the almond extract, and blend 2 minutes until the mixture is creamy and slightly whipped up. Spread the filling in the cooled crust and refrigerate until firm, about 3 hours. (The pie can be prepared to this point one day ahead, covered with plastic wrap, and kept refrigerated until ready to serve.)

A couple of hours before you're ready to serve the pie, arrange the banana slices, then the kiwi slices, in concentric circles from the edge of the crust toward the center. You'll want to leave a circle in the center; place the blackberries in the center. Heat the jam until it's melted and lightly brush the fruit with a thin coating to glaze it. Refrigerate up to 3 hours, or until ready to serve.

Chocolate-Dipped Banana Pops

This is a fun treat for kids to make and eat (actually, adults seem to like them just as much).

Makes 8 servings

8 wooden craft sticks

4 firm-ripe bananas, halved crosswise

1 cup semisweet chocolate chips

2 tablespoons canola oil

Assorted toppings:

candy sprinkles

finely chopped peanuts

sweetened, shredded coconut

M&Ms

toffee bits

Insert the sticks about 1½ inches into the end of each banana half. Place on a large baking sheet lined with wax paper and freeze 1 hour.

In a small saucepan, heat the chocolate chips and oil, stirring until the chocolate melts and becomes smooth; remove from the heat and keep warm. Place each topping on a separate square of wax paper and line them up on a cutting board or a large baking sheet.

Holding the banana pop by the stick over the saucepan, spoon the melted chocolate over the banana, allowing excess to drip back into the pan. Immediately roll the pop in a topping and return to the baking sheet. Repeat with remaining pops. Freeze the pops at least 3 hours or overnight. Let stand for 3 or 4 minutes at room temperature before eating. Frozen pops can be placed in a self-sealing freezer storage bag for up to 1 week.

Variation

White-chocolate banana pops: Melt 1 cup white chocolate chips with 1 tablespoon of oil. Dip pops as described above and roll in chopped cashews, chopped macadamia nuts, or coconut. You can also double-dip the pops: First dip the pops in the dark chocolate and allow it to harden; then dip the top half into white chocolate.

Banana Blondies

Stirred together in a single pan, these chewy, brownie-like bars are a snap to make. The rich banana-butterscotch flavor stands in for the chocolate you're accustomed to in brownies.

Makes sixteen 2-inch squares

6 tablespoons unsalted butter, plus
  more for buttering pan

1^1/$_2$ cups dark brown sugar

1 large egg

1^1/$_2$ teaspoons pure vanilla extract

1 cup mashed ripe banana
  (about 2^1/$_2$ large bananas)

^{1}/$_4$ teaspoon salt

1^1/$_3$ cups all-purpose flour

^{3}/$_4$ cup chopped pecans, toasted

Heat oven to 350°F. Line the bottom of an 8-inch-square pan with waxed paper and butter the bottom and sides.

Melt the butter over low heat in a medium saucepan and add the brown sugar. Bring to a simmer and cook about 1 minute to dissolve the sugar. Allow to cool 10 minutes. Beat in the egg, vanilla, and banana. Stir together the salt and flour, and stir into the batter until just blended; fold in the pecans with a rubber spatula. Pour into the prepared pan.

Bake 35 minutes, or until the blondies just pull away from the sides of the pan. Set the pan on a rack until cool enough to handle. Invert on a rack, peel off the waxed paper, turn right side up, and cool completely. Place on a cutting board and use a sharp knife to cut into squares.

Banana-Oatmeal Cookies

These are the wholesome sort of cookies I think everyone's grandmother must have made. Not too sweet and pleasantly chewy—just the cookie to enjoy with a cup of hot tea. To make them a bit more naughty, try the chocolate-dipped variation.

Makes 2 dozen

1 cup all-purpose flour

³/₄ cup old-fashioned rolled oats

¹/₂ teaspoon ground cinnamon

¹/₂ teaspoon baking powder

¹/₂ teaspoon baking soda

¹/₄ teaspoon salt

¹/₂ cup unsalted butter, room temperature

¹/₂ cup packed light brown sugar

1 large egg

¹/₂ cup mashed ripe banana (about 1¹/₄ bananas)

¹/₂ teaspoon pure vanilla extract

¹/₂ cup chopped pecans

¹/₃ cup currants or raisins, optional

Preheat the oven to 350°F. Lightly spray a cookie sheet with vegetable oil.

Stir together the flour, oats, cinnamon, baking powder, baking soda, and salt. Place the butter and sugar in a large mixing bowl and beat with an electric mixer until light and fluffy. Beat in the egg, banana, and vanilla. Add the flour-oat mixture and mix until just blended. Fold in the pecans and the currants, if using, with a rubber spatula.

Drop the batter by tablespoonfuls onto the prepared cookie sheet, leaving about 1 inch between cookies. Bake about 12 minutes, until the cookies are lightly golden around the edges. Cool 5 minutes before transferring the cookies to racks to cool completely. Cookies will stay fresh in an airtight container up to a week.

Variation

Chocolate-dipped variation: Follow the directions above, cooling cookies completely. Melt 1 cup semisweet or milk chocolate chips in the microwave in a deep ceramic bowl. Dip half of the cookie into the chocolate and transfer to racks until the chocolate dries.

Island Banana Fritters

Bananas are superb marinated in rum and then batter fried. To make an extra-special dessert, serve them in a pool of warm Custard Sauce (page 152).

Makes 4 servings

$^1/_4$ cup dark rum

1 tablespoon fresh lime juice

2 tablespoons brown sugar

4 firm-ripe bananas

1 cup all-purpose baking mix (such as Bisquick)

1 tablespoon granulated sugar

1 cup milk

1 large egg

1 tablespoon butter, melted

Vegetable oil for deep frying

Confectioners' sugar for dusting

Combine the rum, lime juice, and brown sugar in a medium-size bowl. Peel and slice the bananas crosswise into 1$^1/_2$-inch pieces. Toss them in the rum mixture, cover with plastic wrap, and refrigerate 30 minutes.

Place the baking mix, sugar, milk, egg, and butter in a blender and purée on low speed until smooth. Pour the batter into a bowl (if it seems thin, add a tablespoon of Bisquick).

Heat the oil in an electric skillet, deep fryer, or a large pot with a thermometer attached to 375°F. Drain the banana pieces and pat them thoroughly dry with paper towels. Dip about 5 banana pieces at a time into the batter to coat them, then gently slip them into the hot oil, making sure to keep them separate as they cook. Fry until golden on all sides, about 2 minutes per side. Transfer fritters to paper towels to drain, then to a baking sheet in a 200°F oven to keep warm while you cook the rest. Serve them hot, dusted with confectioners' sugar. Makes 20 fritters.

Ambrosia

A Southern mainstay goes tropical with the addition of bananas and fresh coconut. It's wonderful served alongside a plain cake such as Banana Pound Cake (page 121). If you can't find finger bananas, substitute two to three red ones or two regular bananas.

Makes 6 servings

4 large navel oranges

4 to 6 ripe finger bananas, thinly
  sliced lengthwise

¹/3 cup fresh orange juice

2 tablespoons confectioners' sugar

1 tablespoon Cointreau

1 cup fresh coconut shavings, or
  ¹/2 cup sweetened, shredded coconut

With a sharp knife, cut away the rind and white membrane of the oranges. Slice the oranges into thin, crosswise rounds. Layer the oranges and bananas in a glass dish. Mix together the juice, sugar, and Cointreau and drizzle over the fruit. Top with coconut shavings. Chill at least 2 to 3 hours before serving.

Grilled Fruit Brochettes with Rosemary Syrup

Make and serve this fruit dessert following a summer dinner cooked on the grill. You can also use mango or papaya, or any number of firm fruits, depending on what's in season. This is quite delicious on its own but is even better with ice cream or sour cream sprinkled with brown sugar.

Makes 6 servings

³/4 cup mild-flavored honey

1 tablespoon butter

2 tablespoons minced fresh rosemary

1 (2-inch) stick cinnamon

4 firm-ripe bananas

4 red Bartlett pears, or firm-ripe
   peaches or nectarines

1 very ripe pineapple, peeled and cored

Combine the honey, 2 tablespoons water, the butter, rosemary, and cinnamon in a medium saucepan and bring to a boil; lower the heat and simmer 2 minutes. Remove from the heat and allow to cool to room temperature. Strain and set aside.

Cut the ends from the unpeeled bananas and slice into 1½-inch long pieces. Pierce each piece in 2 places to allow steam to escape. Core the pears and cut into 1-inch-thick slices. Cut the pineapple into 2-inch chunks. Thread the fruit pieces alternately onto 6 metal skewers. Brush lightly with the rosemary syrup. Grill or broil over medium-high heat, 2 to 3 minutes per side until lightly browned, basting each time you turn them with more syrup. Arrange on a platter and slip off the banana skins. Drizzle with a bit more syrup and serve warm.

Grilled Banana Splits

My part-time job throughout junior high and high school was at the local DQ, and thanks to little leaguers, I've probably made thousands of banana splits. The Dairy Queen formula was rarely deviated from—except for certain football players—and we were taught to weigh out the custard and ladle precise amounts of topping onto each mound of ice cream. Strawberry syrup was placed in the bow of the plastic boats, pineapple in the center, and chocolate sauce at the stern. Walnut syrup was 25 cents extra, although three maraschino cherries and the Reddi-whip that circled the boat like a lei were included in the 75-cent price.

This is a deviation I've been wanting to try for years. Grilled bananas are far superior to raw—in fact, they're superb! —and freshly made toppings are worth the small effort it takes to stir them up beforehand. Have everything ready before you grill so that the fruit will be hot. Let guests top their sundaes as they wish—it may be the most fun they've had since high school.

Makes 4 servings

Chocolate Rum Sauce (recipe follows)

Butterscotch Sauce (recipe follows)

Walnut Syrup (recipe follows)

$1/2$ cup heavy cream

2 tablespoons confectioners' sugar

4 tablespoons butter, melted

$1/4$ cup packed brown sugar

4 firm-ripe bananas

Vanilla ice cream

Marachino cherries with stems

Make the ice cream toppings and have them ready to serve in bowls. Whip the cream and confectioners' sugar in a large bowl with an electric mixer until it forms stiff peaks. Set aside and keep cool.

Combine the butter and brown sugar in a bowl. Leave the peels on the bananas and slice them in half lengthwise. Brush the cut sides of the bananas with the butter mixture (alternately, you can briefly broil peeled and buttered bananas). Heat the grill to medium-high heat (or prepare charcoal). Grill the bananas, cut side down first, 2 to 3 minutes, or until seared and hot. Transfer to a platter, remove the peels, and brush the other side with the butter mixture. Place 2 banana halves in a large, shallow bowl. Repeat with remaining bananas. Arrange 2 or 3 scoops of vanilla or other ice cream between the banana slices. Spoon on sauces, drizzle with walnut syrup, add a dollop of whipped cream, and place a cherry on top.

Chocolate Rum Sauce

Makes about 1¹/₂ cups

1 cup (6 ounces) semisweet
    chocolate chips

¹/₂ cup heavy cream

2 teaspoons light corn syrup

1 tablespoon dark rum

Heat the chocolate chips, cream, and corn syrup in a metal bowl set
over a pan of barely simmering water (alternately, heat in the microwave for about 1 minute until chocolate is half-melted; remove
and stir until sauce is smooth). Stir in the rum. Keep warm until
ready to serve, or reheat.

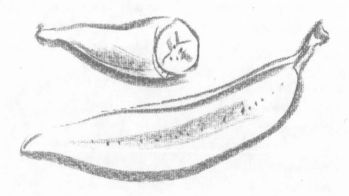

Butterscotch Sauce

Makes about 1¹/₄ cups

¹/₂ cup packed dark brown sugar

¹/₂ cup pure maple syrup

2 tablespoons butter

¹/₄ teaspoon salt

1 teaspoon pure vanilla extract

³/₄ cup half-and-half

Heat the brown sugar and maple syrup in a heavy saucepan over low heat, stirring constantly, until the sugar dissolves. Bring to a boil and cook, stirring, about 5 minutes. Remove from the heat and add the butter, salt, and vanilla. Let stand about 5 minutes. Add the half-and-half and beat 1 or 2 minutes, until it lightens and becomes very creamy. Keep warm until ready to serve.

Walnut Syrup

Makes about 1 cup

1 cup granulated sugar

2 tablespoons dark corn syrup

$^1/_4$ teaspoon pure vanilla extract

$^1/_2$ cup chopped walnuts, lightly toasted

Heat the sugar, $^1/_2$ cup water, and the corn syrup in a heavy saucepan over low heat. Stir until the sugar is dissolved. Bring to a boil and cook, without stirring, 3 minutes, or until just slightly thick. Remove from the heat and cool 1 minute. Stir in the vanilla and walnuts. Keep warm until ready to serve.

What's a Banana Republic?

Before the khaki-peddling retail clothing giant came on the scene, a banana republic was (and still is) a term used to describe a small state, often Central American, run by a despot dependent on the fruit exporting trade as well as the support of American banana companies keenly interested in maintaining community relations in the region. Sometimes the American government even lent a hand in maintaining those relationships. For example, when a left-leaning president of Guatemala appropriated land in the 1950s owned by the United Fruit Company (now Chiquita), he was overthrown in an infamous coup backed by the Central Intelligence Agency.

Banana-Maple Ice Cream

You can make a pure fruit sorbet simply by freezing bananas and whirring them in a food processor. Add a few more ingredients, and it becomes a special frozen dessert that you can make without an ice cream maker.

Makes 4 servings

6 ripe bananas

$1/2$ cup pure maple syrup

$1^1/2$ teaspoons pure vanilla extract

$1/3$ cup heavy cream

Pinch of salt

Peel the bananas and freeze them in a self-sealing storage bag 5 hours or overnight. Slice the frozen bananas and place them in the bowl of a food processor along with the maple syrup, vanilla, cream, and salt. Purée until smooth, pour into an 8-inch-square baking dish and re-freeze until solid, 1 or 2 hours. Cut the ice cream into pieces and return to the food processor. Purée until creamy, 1 or 2 minutes. Serve immediately.

Banana-Pear Sorbet

This fat-free sorbet starts with a can of fruit and has a surprisingly smooth texture and fresh taste that is often lacking in store-bought fruit sorbets. You can also use canned peaches or pineapple with the bananas—keep a few cans in your freezer for a quick, frosty treat.

Makes 6 servings

2 (16-ounce) cans sliced or halved pears in heavy syrup

2 ripe bananas, frozen

2 tablespoons fresh lime juice

2 tablespoons dark rum

Freeze the unopened cans of pears until solid, at least 18 hours. Submerge the frozen can in hot water for 1 minute. Open the can and slide out the contents onto a cutting board. Using a very sharp knife, slice into 1-inch-thick slices, then into large chunks, and place them in the bowl of a food processor. Slice the banana and add to the processor, along with the lime juice and rum. Process, pulsing on and off, until smooth. Serve immediately or transfer to a storage container and freeze until ready to serve.

Banana, Mango, and Ginger Chutney

Mango, ginger, and serrano chile add a tangy bite to this savory banana chutney. Slather it on roast pork, grilled chicken, or a ham sandwich.

Makes 2¹/₂ cups

1 cup white vinegar

¹/₂ cup packed brown sugar

1 cup orange juice

2 cups diced firm-ripe banana (about 4 bananas)

1 ripe mango, peeled and diced

1¹/₂ tablespoons grated gingerroot

1 serrano chile with seeds, minced

1 teaspoon salt

¹/₂ cup golden raisins

1 stick cinnamon

¹/₂ teaspoon ground nutmeg

¹/₂ teaspoon ground allspice

¹/₂ teaspoon ground white pepper

Pinch of cayenne

Bring vinegar to a boil in a large nonaluminum pan. Stir in brown sugar and orange juice and return to a boil. Reduce heat to low and simmer 10 minutes. Stir in remaining ingredients and bring to a simmer. Cook, stirring, 25 to 30 minutes, or until chutney has thickened. Cool and remove cinnamon stick. The chutney will keep up to six months stored in jars with tight-fitting lids.

Green Banana and Date Conserve

Sweetened with dates and crystallized ginger, this chunky condiment is good with cold chicken or grilled meats. Use bananas that are just a day or two from turning completely yellow.

Makes about 3 cups

1 cup cider vinegar

1 cup unsweetened pineapple juice

$1/2$ cup packed light brown sugar

6 green-tipped bananas, coarsely
   mashed

1 cup chopped dates

$1/4$ cup minced crystallized ginger

1 teaspoon curry powder

$1/4$ teaspoon salt

$1/4$ cup slivered almonds

Combine the vinegar, pineapple juice, and brown sugar in a nonreactive saucepan and bring to a boil. Add the remaining ingredients, except the almonds, and cook over low heat, stirring until the chutney has a jamlike consistency. Remove from the heat and cool to room temperature. Stir in the almonds. The chutney will keep for 3 weeks in a jar, refrigerated.

Tropical Barbecue Sauce

Adding crushed pineapple, banana, and a few other tasty ingredients to a basic tomato barbecue sauce transforms it into a sensational marinade for grilled chicken, pork chops, or ribs.

Makes about 2¹/₂ cups

2 tablespoons vegetable oil

1 cup finely chopped red onion

4 ripe bananas, mashed

¹/₂ cup Heinz ketchup

¹/₂ cup red wine vinegar

¹/₂ cup crushed pineapple

¹/₄ cup packed dark brown sugar

¹/₄ cup mild-flavored molasses

1 tablespoon soy sauce

2 to 3 teaspoons habañero or other
    Caribbean-style hot sauce

1 tablespoon dark rum

Heat the oil in a large saucepan over medium heat. Add the onion and cook until soft. Combine the remaining sauce ingredients, except the rum, and bring to a boil. Lower the heat and simmer, stirring occasionally, about 20 to 30 minutes, or until the sauce is thick. Stir in the rum and cook 1 minute more. For a smoother sauce, purée in a blender. The sauce will keep, refrigerated, for 2 weeks.

Sources

Fresh and dried bananas

Frieda's
4465 Corporate Center Drive
Los Alamitos, CA 90720
(800) 241–1771
www.friedas.com
*Fresh banana leaves as well as Burro, Ice
Cream, Manzano, Niño, Plantain, and
Red bananas*

Melissa's
P.O. Box 21127
Los Angeles, CA 90021
www.melissas.com
(800) 588–0151
*Varieties including Burro, Manzano, Niño,
Plantain, and Red, as well as dried banana
chips and sun-dried bananas*

Banana plants and seeds

These two nurseries specialize in banana
plants, but there are many more sources
on the worldwide web.

Going Bananas
24401 S.W. 197th Avenue
Homestead, FL 33031
www.goingbananas.com
(305) 247–0397
*Nearly 100 varieties of banana plants,
including dessert and cooking bananas,
plantains, and ornamental varieties*

The Banana Tree
715 Northampton Street
Easton, PA 18042
www.banana-tree.com
(610) 253–9589
Seeds for fruiting and ornamental bananas

Books

Sadly, most books on the history of bananas and cultivation are out of print. You may be able to find some of these through secondhand dealers or through Amazon.com. You can also get general cultivating information from many tropical gardening books.

Abella, Alex. *The Total Banana.* New York: Harcourt Brace Jovanovich, 1979.

Lessard, William O. *The Complete Book of Bananas.* Self-published, 1992.

Organizations

The Banana Museum
1222 K Street, N.E.
Auburn, WA 98002
(253) 833-8043
www.geocities.com/NapaValley/1799
Banana collector Ann Lovell has turned her home into a museum. She loves to share her enthusiasm with others and opens her house to visitors by appointment only.

The International Banana Club
2524 North El Molino Avenue
Altadena, CA 91001
www.banana-club.com
A philanthropic club and museum with an international membership. Membership is $25 (they sometimes run specials), and you can sign up by mail or through the internet.

Bibliography

Anderson, Jean, and Elaine Hanna. *The New Doubleday Cookbook: The Basic Cookbook for the Complete Kitchen.* New York: Doubleday, 1985.

Barber, Mary Corpening, Sara Corpening, and Lori Lyn Narlock. *Smoothies: 50 Recipes for High-Energy Refreshment.* San Francisco: Chronicle Books, 1997.

Cordova, Regina, with Emma Carrasco for The National Council of La Raza. *Celebración: Recipes & Traditions Celebrating Latino Family Life.* New York: Main Street Books, 1996.

Creen, Linette. *A Taste of Cuba: Recipes from the Cuban-American Community.* New York: Plume, 1994.

Gorman, Marion. *Cooking with Fruit.* Emmaus, PA: Rodale Press, 1983.

Hachten, Harvan. *Best of Regional African Cooking.* New York: Hippocrene Books, Inc., 1998.

Harris, Jessica B. *Iron Pots & Wooden Spoons: Africa's Gifts to New World Cooking.* New York: Fireside, 1999.

———*Sky Juice and Flying Fish: Traditional Caribbean Cooking.* New York: Fireside, 1991.

Karoff, Barbara. *South American Cooking: Foods and Feasts from the New World.* Berkeley: Aris Books, 1989.

Kotkin, Carole, and Kathy Martin. *MMMMiami: Tempting Tropical Tastes for Home Cooks Everywhere.* New York: Henry Holt, 1998.

LaFray, Joyce. *Cuba Cocina!: The Tantalizing World of Cuban Cooking—Yesterday, Today, and Tomorrow*. New York: William Morrow, 1994.

Lessard, W. O. *The Complete Book of Bananas*. Self-published, 1992.

Lindquist, Carol. *The Banana Lover's Cookbook*. New York: St. Martin's Press, 1993.

Malgieri, Nick. *How to Bake*. New York: HarperCollins, 1995.

Marks, Copeland. *False Tongues and Sunday Bread: A Guatemalan and Mayan Cookbook*. New York: M. Evans, 1985.

Ortiz, Elizabeth Lambert. *The Book of Latin American Cooking*. Hopewell, NJ: The Ecco Press, 1994.

Rivera, Oswald. *Puerto Rican Cuisine in America: Nuyorican and Bodega Recipes*. New York: Four Walls Eight Windows, 1993.

Routhier, Nicole. *Fruit Cookbook: 400 Sweet and Savory, Fruit-Filled Recipes, Soups to Desserts*. New York: Workman, 1996.

Schneider, Elizabeth. *Uncommon Fruits & Vegetables: A Commonsense Guide*. New York: Harper & Row, 1986.

Young, Joyce LaFray. *Tropic Cooking*. Berkeley: Ten Speed Press, 1987.

Index